Praise for
Guilt Free

"Guilt Free: Using Remorse to Espcape the Adversary's Tool is an insightful look at the negative effects of guilt in our lives. Through sharing personal and professional experiences, Karen illustrates the importance of having a positive attitude and learning from our mistakes, not punishing ourselves for them. Karen gently reminds us that real happiness is not something that is given to us; it requires substantial effort. This book shares sound doctrinal principles and examples of how people have used these principles to overcome the effects of guilt. *Guilt Free* is easy to read, understand, and be inspired by. I would highly recommend this book."

—**Dan Hymas**, CPRP, CECP; business manager, Upper Valley Resource & Counseling Center

"This book is tremendous in helping us understanding not only others, but also ourselves. It shows better ways to look at ourselves and others. But for me what sets this book apart from so many others is its insight into guilt and remorse, the difference between them, and the necessity of one and destructiveness of the other, all the while showing the effect these feelings can have in applying the Atonement. Thanks for taking the steps to follow your inspiration in writing this book, Karen!"

—**Dr. Michael R. Merrell**, DDS

"Karen teaches a refreshing and effective approach to emotional wellness centered on the Atonement of Jesus Christ. Readers will find her analogies and personal anecdotes interesting and helpful in understanding the ideas she presents. I believe peace can be found by following the concepts she so clearly promotes."

—**Reed Stoddard**, LMSW, director of BYU–I Counseling Center

"An essential read in self-help literature, *Guilt Free* strings together bite-sized nuggets of useful tips excised from real-world stories gleaned from the author's years of experience in the field of counseling. The book is interesting to read, easy to understand, and laced with solid techniques from which to build on and improve one's situation. The material is presented in such a way that it is intriguing as a read-once book, but it has the added advantage of providing value for years to come as it is perused and further studied."

—**Jim Clark**, Salem, Idaho, radio station manager

"*Guilt Free* is an engaging treatise that explores the impact of remorse versus guilt in the lives of people. The material is enlivened by life stories, practical experience, observations and insights. An enjoyable read and a "how to" for more peaceful living."

—**Enid Lee Davis**, LCPC, LSW, EdD

DISHONEST
WRONG
UNBECOMING
SIN
FAULT
ACCUSATION
GUILT
FREE
REGRET
FALSE
DISHONOR
GUILTY
UNWORTHY
FLAW
FAKE
GUILT
LAPSE
LIE
SELF-WORTH
FLAGRANT

USING REMORSE TO ESCAPE
THE ADVERSARY'S TOOL

KAREN JOHN

CFI
An Imprint of Cedar Fort, Inc.
Springville, Utah

ISBN 13: 978-1-4621-1410-8

Published by CFI, an imprint of Cedar Fort, Inc.
2373 W. 700 S., Springville, UT 84663
Distributed by Cedar Fort, Inc., www.cedarfort.com

LIBRARY OF CONGRESS CATALOGING-IN-PUBLICATION DATA

John, Karen W., 1956- author.
Guilt free / Karen W. John.
    pages cm
Summary: Explains the important difference between guilt and remorse and how Lucifer uses guilt to manipulate and destroy our self-esteem.
ISBN 978-1-4621-1410-8
1. Guilt--Religious aspects--Church of Jesus Christ of Latter-day Saints. 2. Self-esteem--Religious aspects--Church of Jesus Christ of Latter-day Saints. 3. Mormons--Conduct of life. I. Title.

BX8656.J58 2014
233'.4--dc23

                              2013045970

Cover design by Shawnda T. Craig
Cover design © 2014 Lyle Mortimer
Edited and typeset by Kevin Haws

Printed in Canada

10 9 8 7 6 5 4 3 2 1

Printed on acid-free paper

Contents

Book One: Recognizing Our Limitations

1

The Knock at My Bedroom Door

I **will never** forget one particular morning when I heard a soft knock on my bedroom door. At the other side was my teenage son. He hesitantly said, "Mom, I have a stomachache."

This scenario was getting all too familiar, so I answered gently, "Honey, what's wrong? How come you don't like school?" He began to cry and answered with his head down, "Because I'm not good at it."

"Sweetheart," I said, "you don't have to be good at it. The winner is the one who just keeps trying. Heavenly Father doesn't expect us to be good at everything. He just wants us to keep trying."

How does a young teenager, or anyone for that matter, get to this point? It could be this young man has older brothers whom he might be comparing himself to, or maybe school friends who seem to handle the pressure of education better than he believes he does. This kind of negative, self-defeating thinking becomes common as we live our lives, as the people and situations around us affect us in numerous ways; sadly, these types of thoughts negatively target our self-esteem.

The adversary focuses on these negative thoughts and feelings, expanding them by any means he can. His goal is to make us feel horrible about ourselves. He wants us to give up, exactly the opposite of what Christ wants for us—what Christ gives us. The Savior is encouraging and loving. He never gives up on us.

Christ and the adversary both understand the nature of our mortality. They understand that it's normal for us to not feel "good enough" while here on earth. Christ's goal is to encourage us to keep going whereas the adversary's goal is the complete opposite: he wants us to give up.

The adversary recognizes human weaknesses and targets them to make us feel worse. How does this happen and, more important, how can we change the way we feel? The first step in the process is identifying how we feel by asking certain questions.

Not Feeling Good Enough? Welcome to the Human Race!

- Have you ever felt that you're not good enough?
- Do you feel guilty for things you have done or haven't done?
- Is the negative energy inside of you so buried that it's become hard to identify?
- Do you question why you can't access or get rid of these unwanted feelings?
- Have you wondered what might be behind these feelings and why they linger when they're not wanted?

Okay, if you answered yes to any of these questions, welcome to the human race! You're normal; everyone struggles with these feelings until they have the opportunity to be healed through Christ. So if you have felt these feelings or are currently struggling with some of them, you are normal. Why don't we feel good enough? Why do we hold onto feelings of unresolved pain, guilt, and shame? After all, we're taught that we are literal children of God. Should we not be feeling the peace of our magnificent, royal heritage instead of pain and guilt? Does it seem that sometimes we miss the happiness in the plan of happiness? Is it part of the journey, part of growth? How do we as humans build such toxicity inside of us without desiring to do so?

Pain builds for several reasons because we have mortal human natures, which feel different than our celestial spirits, feelings of guilt and shame grow, especially during our youth when our ability to reason is limited. As we develop, the feelings begin to produce turmoil and anxiety. Feelings of peace fade. We instead feel lethargic and unloved. Not good enough. Toxic.

Why can't we let go of these toxic feelings? After all, we resist pain because we don't like experiencing it. So we stuff the pain down instead, as far inside as we can, and we continue to keep it out of sight, out of mind. However, pain doesn't go away until we are willing to work through it.

Another reason we can't let pain go is that we have been conditioned through society to hide our emotions and feelings. We live in a non-attached society. If you're like most people, it's difficult to find even one or two others whom you could trust with everything. This condition isn't what Christ would have us live in. We are taught to "mourn with those that mourn; yea, and comfort those that stand in need of comfort" (Mosiah 18:9). This includes ourselves and those whom we are closest to: our spouses, family members, and so on. We all need to have a soft, safe place to land at the end of the day, especially with the unpredictable events of our society and the world in general.

Society has also taught us that emotional expression is a sign of weakness. We are told to be strong, to move forward without acknowledging and processing through our emotions. Christ didn't teach this when He walked the earth.

While here, Christ accomplished three main tasks. First, and most important, He atoned for the sins of all humanity. He saved us from both physical death and eternal spiritual death. Otherwise, we would have been forever stuck in darkness with the adversary.

Our life here on earth is like a field of muck and mud where we would sink down with each step without Christ's Atonement. As we focus on Christ at the end of the field of mud, He lovingly pulls each of us out and tenderly washes us so that we enter into the most beautiful existence imaginable: our next estate.

Second, He taught us everything we need to know to return and reside with Him forever in His beautiful garden.

And third, He healed us. He relieves us of emotional and physical pain when our hope, energy, and faith are directed toward Him. He heals everyone through His light, which shines in every living thing. Christ was not a respecter of persons (see D&C 38:16), so the healing that was available to the people who literally walked with Christ is just as accessible to us now. Christ is the source of all light. We can access that light for healing purposes in our own lives. Our power is great if we choose to follow Christ and His teachings.

Pain is a part of life. We came to earth to learn, and in doing so we experience a lot of pain and hardship through our trials and adversity. At one point or another, we will hurt, which can change our lives and control our thoughts and actions until we find a source of healing. Some of the consequences to our behaviors and decisions can damage our self-esteem because we start to beat ourselves up for making mistakes and often for simply being human. But our lives can change, for the better if we seek the correct source of healing.

Because of our natural aversion to pain and our societal conditioning, feelings of guilt and past emotional pain can remain inside and end up controlling our daily actions, mostly without our awareness and knowledge. Until we take the necessary steps to access and heal from the known and unknown causes of this ongoing negative energy, or at least obtain the necessary skills to manage our emotions in a healthy and functional manner, we will continue to be in pain.

An additional reason that we hold onto guilt is we compare ourselves to the Lord's standard and realize our shortcomings related to that standard. "When comparing one's personal performance with the supreme standard of the Lord's expectation, the reality of imperfection can at times be depressing. My heart goes out to conscientious Saints who, because of their shortcomings, allow feelings of depression to rob them of happiness in life. We all need to remember: men are that they might have joy—not guilt trips!"[1] Joy should be one of our daily goals and feelings. Heavenly Father explained this concept and how it is possible for us through the scriptures.

Lucifer is working overtime, wanting each of us to believe we're not worth the time required to heal and feel better about ourselves. Lucifer knows and understands the power of guilt and how he can easily manipulate it for his purposes of personal and collective destruction, if we allow him to accomplish this task. We need to be aware of how guilt works so that we can disarm any of Lucifer's influences and employ the healing power of Christ.

As mentioned above, because of our mortality, feelings of guilt continue to build without our recognition, healing, or relief; these feelings can often overwhelm us and take over our lives. When guilt takes over, we become entrenched in these feelings without any apparent escape route. The guilt can and will eventually lead to feelings of inadequacy, depleting or destroying our self-esteem and self-worth. This is Lucifer's goal. Many of us struggle with these negative emotions on a daily basis, which is normal and human. Often we don't understand how we feel or what is behind what we are feeling.

One constant that I have witnessed in individuals whom I have counseled is they feel guilt on some level. I have never worked with anyone who believes they are good enough in every aspect, or sometimes in any aspect, of their lives.

In my experience, behind this incorrect, negative perception of ourselves is that we lack education and understanding of what's truly fueling this pain and guilt. And as hard as we may try to release this pain, it can seem impossible.

The good news is we do have a choice! We do have power through Christ to overcome guilt and pain. This power and light are both easily accessible and constantly available to us. We can either be filled with the light that comes from Jesus Christ's sacrifice or filled with the darkness that comes from Lucifer's use of guilt. The adversary wants us to remember clearly all of our sins and uses guilt to keep these sins in our minds and hearts so that we can't be healed.

Nothing could be further from the truth. We can be healed. We continually learn as individuals and as a society the importance of expressing our feelings for optimal emotional and physical health.

Elder Jeffrey R. Holland warned,

> The world around you is an increasingly hostile and sinful place. Occasionally that splashes onto us, and perhaps, in the case of a few of you, it may be nearly drowning you . . . You can change. You can be helped. You can be made whole—whatever the problem. All He asks is that you *walk away from darkness and come into the light,* His light, with meekness and lowliness of heart. . . . Christ has "borne our griefs, and carried our sorrows," Isaiah declared, "and with His stripes we are healed"—if we want to be (Isaiah 53:4–5; Mosiah 14:4–5).[2]

Sister Elaine Marshall added that because of our limitations with our mortality involving pain and suffering, Christ's ministry on earth involved a lot of healing.

> As Jesus healed, the scriptures say, "All the people were amazed" (Matthew 12:23). They brought their sick, their "blind, and dumb" (Matthew 12:22), those that were "possessed with a devil" (Matthew 12:22; also Mark 1:32), and their dead. They sought Him every day and into the evening. So great was His reputation and His healing power that they sought to "only touch the hem of His garment; and as many touched were made perfectly whole" (Matthew 14:36). "And Jesus went about all the cities and villages, teaching . . . and preaching the gospel . . . and healing every sickness and every disease among the people" (Matthew 9:35). . . . When the Savior appeared in the Americas, He healed "every one as they were brought forth unto Him" (3 Nephi 17:9).[3]

How Guilt Is Built: A Cycle of Buried Pain

Up to this point, we've looked at the reason *why* we, as humans, continue to hold onto toxic energy inside us, and how healing is possible through Christ. But now let's look at *how* this negative energy might have gotten there in the first place.

We feel guilt and pain because our limited brain development restricts our ability to reason during childhood. Our brains don't fully develop until we are approximately twenty-five years old.[4] That's why a teenager can look like an adult, but reasoning ability is still limited. In this stage of development, teenagers can't see beyond themselves, think they're invincible, live in the moment, and cannot fully see the consequences of their actions. This does not take consequences away from our choices and behaviors, but it helps us learn from our decisions and the natural consequences of our decisions.

Children are egocentric, meaning they have a really strong aptitude for making everything about them and making things their fault, even when the situation doesn't necessarily have anything to do with the child.[5] As children, we also misinterpreted other situations on a regular basis with societal influences such as friends, church, school, siblings, teachers, bullies, abusers, and others. Most of us were not willing to accept this reality. Probably over ninety percent of the individuals I have worked with believed that they had a great or "normal" childhood. It is often difficult for us to acknowledge the reality that much of our childhood involved pain. We want to believe we had a great childhood, and for most of us much of our childhood was indeed wonderful. But along with the good, it is important to recognize that all of us internalized a lot of pain and guilt during childhood because of our brain's inability to reason during those years. It's impossible to escape the reality of this pain because, until we heal and process through these feelings, guilt's pain will remain inside of us.

In my experience with healing and helping others, the first step is awareness. If we are not willing to recognize the pain that happened to us in our past, we will not be able to heal and move forward. I would like to illustrate how easily this can happen with some examples and stories.

Let's imagine, for example, that I'm an eight-year-old child who asks for a doll for my birthday and my mother says, "It's kind of expensive, but we will see what we can do." And then, I have a wonderful birthday party and get my coveted doll. I'm so happy, but as I'm brushing her hair quietly I hear my parents arguing over money in the other room. They do not realize that I'm within earshot.

Remember, children are egocentric, which means the world revolves around them and they also have a phenomenal knack to make things their own fault. So I would say to myself, "Look what I have done because I wanted this doll. I want to take her back so they have the money they need for food!" My eight-year-old brain's reasoning ability cannot process through the fact that the doll's price is so minimal compared to their money problems. But I do have the ability to make it my fault. I internalize my feelings of stupidity and tell myself that I'm stupid, selfish, and unworthy for a long time, thus effectively decreasing my self-worth and self-esteem.

This biological limitation leads to all children getting hurt, taking on the pain of situations belonging to others, none of it necessarily their fault. Because of a child's age, limited understanding, and their inability to reason, even the best parents can hurt their children.

Children equate quality time spent with them as love. They don't equate words with love the way most adults might. To illustrate this fact, if I were to call my husband in the middle of his work day and tell him that I just called to say that I loved him, he would feel pretty special and loved for at least a few hours, if not days.

In contrast, if my eight-year-old grandson, Carson, came to visit me and I said, "Carson, I love you so much," he would probably quickly respond with a learned and mannerly, "I love you too, Grandma." But in the same breath, he would ask me where the toys and games were and if I would play with him. He recognizes my willingness to play with him as an expression of love. It is his language of love at his age.

Parents want to be good parents. They do what they believe is best for their children. To illustrate this, suppose there's a father who spends a lot of time with his son. He takes him fishing, hiking, camping, and so on. He spends time carving pumpkins with him on Halloween and decorating Christmas cookies for the neighbors. All of these actions express love to the young child because time equals love for children. One day, this father explains to his son that he is going to teach him how to mow the lawn. The little boy is so excited, because he enjoys being with his dad even if it is work. The boy is eager as his father shows him how to mow the grass in straight lines and how to get all of the corners neatly trimmed.

Following the mowing lesson, the little boy exclaims that he can't wait until he's big enough to mow the lawn by himself. Finally he is. He starts mowing the lawn to surprise his dad, making sure the rows are straight and getting every corner, like his father taught him. He eagerly awaits his father's return home to inspect his efforts. He keeps watching the clock, anticipating his father's return. His father finally pulls up to the curb, but he's had a horrible day at work: he didn't get lunch, he had an argument with his boss, and he experienced road rage on the way home. So he is not in a good mood. He opens the car door and the little boy immediately pops up his head and says, "Dad, I'm mowing the lawn!" His father shuts the door and yells, "Well, don't forget to sweep off the walk!"

That little boy was crushed. He internalized that experience as something he did wrong and the fact that he wasn't good enough.

He cannot understand what his father has been through that day. He is unable to reason through what happened, and because of his egocentric nature he internalized the event of his father's curt response as something that was his fault.

Another area where parents can hurt their children unintentionally is the essential understanding that children are an extension of their parents. Because of this parents expect them to behave in a certain way and accomplish specific goals. Children have difficulty feeling that it is all right to be anything different from these family expectations. They feel the disapproval or push toward compliance when they behave inappropriately.

Healthy conditioning and expectations are essential in raising children. It is the expectation of our Heavenly Father as He trusted us to guide and raise some of His beautiful children that we will love and nurture them in appropriate ways. It's important to note that a definite difference exists between healthy conditioning and expectations, which lead to positive growth and success for children, and unhealthy and abusive expectations, which are always more about the parent than the child. In my experiences with family counseling, punishment is generally about the parent, especially if it is linked with anger. Discipline is about the child because it is associated with teaching the child something he or she needs to know to be able to thrive in today's society with a healthy and functional skill base.

One of my heroes in life was my first boss. He taught me an important lesson about the difference between discipline and punishment. I grew up right in the middle of nine children, so my parents and older siblings often had to raise their voices just to get the younger children's attention. As a result, I would get yelled at a lot if I did something wrong and I would yell a lot to get attention. I thought this was pretty normal until I learned differently. My first boss gave me my initial experience with this concept.

I once worked in the clothes department of a local department store chain. I was excited for my position and the possibility of making some of my own money. I was a ready and willing employee with lots of energy to tackle anything my boss put in front of me. One day he placed two big boxes near a clothes rack and explained that he wanted me to hang up the clothes from the first box using the hangers in the other box onto the clothes rack. That was going to be easy. I got one hanger out and one shirt and began to unbutton the shirt so I would be able to place it on the hanger. My boss stopped me and said, "Karen, do you want to see a cool trick?" I said I did, so he took a shirt from the box and one hanger from the other box and, without unbuttoning one shirt button, he turned the hanger sideways and put it down through the neck of the shirt and brought the hook part of the hanger back up through the neck. I said, "Wow, that's going to save a lot of time!" He said, smiling, "You think?"

My boss was willing to take the time to teach me a new skill instead of saying something like, 'Let me show you how to do that. Your way is going to take all day!' I will forever be grateful to him for taking the time to teach me an important life lesson about respecting others, even if they're children or subordinates in a working environment. There is always an effective way to teach without harming self-worth or self-esteem. It takes more effort, education, and self-control than reacting to our emotions as we try to parent effectively.

Maxine Murdock explains how parents can often get into a reactionary role, which can become more about the parent than the child.

> Sometimes parents with unrealistic expectations of perfection say such things as "Don't you realize you are disgracing the family name? Remember, you are a Jones." Comments like these have nothing to do with the child's worth as a child of God. Other comments may be more subtle, but can still cause deep emotional pain. "How could you hurt your mother like this?" "How do you ever expect to get married if you don't lose a little weight?" Even when the individuals making such comments have the best intentions, they give children feelings of inferiority that may last for years.[6]

My father is a personal example of this truth. As a child, he was raised in an extremely strict home. His father was so strict he even told my father that it was mandatory that he became a lawyer, and my father's brother was to become a physician. My father didn't have any desire to be a lawyer, but he was afraid to speak up because expressing emotion was not acceptable in my father's childhood home. When his father expressed emotion it was all too often with inappropriate anger. My father became afraid of him and his reactions. By the time my father was sixteen years old he developed bleeding ulcers because of the constant stress resulting from the pressure he felt in his home and the resulting fear of his father. He was almost through with law school before he was brave enough to explain to his father that he did not want to be a lawyer. This inability to express emotions in a healthy and functional way was passed on to my family home with less intensity. My father's parenting abilities were limited because he was not able to express appropriate, vulnerable emotions during his childhood formative years.

As a result of him not having a safe place to express pain and vulnerability, my experience with him as his daughter was mostly one of fear as he often was only able to communication using anger, harsh words, and occasionally physical punishment.

My intention here is not to beat upon or berate parents. My intention is for parents to not feel guilt over being human. All of us are parents or children dealing with this same issue that mortality presents. All of us make mistakes! All parents hurt their children. The pain that is generated from parents is almost always unintentional and it is never the intention of the child to assimilate the pain. Because the world revolves around them, children internalize some situations that might not have a single thing to do with them. In addition, parents might only be a small part of childhood pain.

Another example where we may experience pain is our schooling years. This can happen with friends or bullies who tease and abuse us. Sadly, sometimes it can even be through our authority figures such as teachers.

One example that has affected my husband's self-esteem happened in a classroom during his early childhood years. He remembers, "When I was in kindergarten or first grade, I had a problem pronouncing some words and sounds. My teacher was determined to help me get over this problem and brought me up to the front of the class for an 'accelerated' learning experience. I could not pronounce the TW sound in the word twenty. Instead, I would say *quenty*, with a Q sound.

"My teacher then said, 'Byron, say the word *twenty*.' I said 'quenty' and the whole class laughed at me. She made me stay in front of the class trying to pronounce twenty for probably thirty to forty attempts. I finally did say it correctly, but for the first time in my life, I felt total public humiliation at the hands of an authority figure. Since that day, I have had a mistrust of speaking in front of authority figures for fear of saying something wrong."

This incident happened within one half-hour. That short a period of time, and yet my husband's self-esteem and self-concept is still affected to this day. We learn through these painful childhood experiences that we're not good enough learn the lesson well.

Learning to Stop the Cycle

The sad part about this education is that it's false. To illustrate how much influence our childhood experiences have on our self-esteem, visualize yourself as a newborn baby. I want you to feel how innocent and pure you feel. You were once the same way.

Now, let's grow up a little bit and become an active two-year-old. If you can imagine a two-year-old's self-esteem and self-concept regarding how wonderful and deserving they believe they are for a minute with me, then we can understand that they have no problem expressing to anyone what they want and what they feel they need. They know that they deserve it and demand attention to get it. These little guys or girls feel their divine nature daily. They know they deserve to take up their entitled space on earth. They accomplish tasks full steam ahead, without any hesitation. If they draw a picture, they know it is a beautiful picture. All of us were two-year-olds at one point in time. All of us knew we deserved to be loved and to have our needs met.

Ask yourself: do you know what a two-year-old knows? Do you have confidence to accomplish tasks without fear? If you are like many of us, you doubt your abilities and your worthiness. You have a difficult time feeling you are good enough. The things that you do might not be enough. So what happened?

What happened is that our community, the people surrounding us influenced our self-concept and self-esteem, often in a negative manner. When we are young, we don't have the biological ability to reason through and direct the messages sent our way back to the original source. We don't have the knowledge or understanding of the truth behind the messages. Instead we internalize the message as truth regarding ourselves. These are learned negative messages; they are not innate.

To understand how this happens, picture yourself as a flower in the middle of garden of flowers. Realize that you're naturally influenced by the garden elements surrounding you such as the water, sun, weeds, fertilizer, and so on. In life, these elements are your community and society in general, your religion and your interactions with fellow church members, your parents, your siblings, and your school experience including friends and bullies.

Next, make a list of all the messages you tell yourself every day. After you have finished your list, identify where those messages came from. All of the messages did indeed come from these elements surrounding and affecting you. Were these messages positive, contributing to your growth and self-esteem? Or were they negative?

If they were negative messages, they have everything to do with the elements, not with you. These elements were human beings in your life with imperfections like you. The negative messages you continue to tell yourself came from external factors, made up of flawed human beings. These dysfunctional messages belong to the people who gave them to you and don't have anything to do with you.

We assimilate what we have learned from the elements around us because these external factors are close to us in proximity. These elements affect us daily and will continue to do so. They have the ability to either contribute to our growth and self-esteem or to destroy it. It's important to understand that there's a big difference between our adult brains and our childhood brains. As an adult, we often have the ability to effectively reason through our daily circumstances. We can look at the situation clearly and work through it, possibly deflecting potential pain when necessary for self-preservation. This wasn't possible for us when we were children. We internalized the messages because that's all we knew how to do at the time.

Now, visualize yourself giving those messages back to the external influences that they belong to, the ones that taught you the messages in the first place. These messages don't belong to you. They never will. They never have, and they're probably getting pretty heavy after lugging them around for so long.

Let's look at a situation that illustrates this point. Imagine a young woman who was being teased in school because she had a problem with acne for a few years. She might be rejected by her friends because of this condition. If so, she then internalized the fact that she is not good enough, not pretty enough. She might even consider herself ugly. This message becomes part of her self-concept. But probably none of what she internalized was truth.

Someone might try to talk to her about her friends' negative behaviors, explaining the fact that it has nothing to do with her. Talking about the issue is definitely helpful for her thinking process, but until she can heal from these painful feelings and express her sadness in a safe environment, these emotions will continue to fuel negative self-talk, which can create feelings of guilt for not being good enough.

Because we can't reason in a healthy and functional way, and we have not always been allowed or encouraged to express our painful emotions, we've learned to internalize them. These internalized emotions become hard and unidentifiable. They are the source and power behind our ongoing pain and negative self-esteem.

Self-Preservation and Protection

When we have been hurt too much, we metaphorically place our hearts in a safe with a strong lock, and then we put on a steel vest with twelve combination locks, holding our arms out in front of us to deflect any pain that might come near us. We become alienated when hiding our emotions from others.

An unknown author once said,

> No matter how much you love someone, no matter how much you want them to be happy, no matter how much you believe in who they are, your love and desire for their happiness will not be enough . . . the love that one gives to someone who does not believe he is lovable or believe in his divine nature will be greeted with a cool rebuff. It will be as though hundreds of arrows were shot, not one piercing the warmth of the soul, but rather each meeting an impenetrable wall; a wall that both protects and imprisons.[7]

How might we be able to penetrate these walls around ourselves and those whom we love? Robert C. Oaks explains how important it is for us to get to know ourselves.

> For us to move in the desired direction for our own lives, we must come to know ourselves. We must study, stretch, and test ourselves and ponder the results. This getting-to-know-yourself process is important because it enables you to do more with your life. It permits you to come closer to realizing your full potential. It lets you build on and use your strengths, your gifts, and your talents to carry out your purpose in God's plan.[8]

Coming to know ourselves is crucial. The part of ourselves we tend to resist is our mortal natures. Acceptance of our limited and carnal nature of mortality is one of the first steps needed toward positive growth and progression in our ultimate quest to be like our Heavenly Father. Becoming like our Heavenly Father is a journey taken step by step, and it begins with self-awareness.

Alifeleti Malupo of The Church of Jesus Christ of Latter-day Saints is director of the LDS Social Services Agency in Honolulu, Hawaii. He explained, "It is hard for most people to understand why they do what they do. In many situations, people think that someone else made them do it. They thus feel justified doing whatever it may be; they never take the time to learn or to understand why they really do what they do. I always advise people to take time to learn about themselves. The better they know and truly understand themselves the better and sooner they can help themselves."[9]

Acceptance of our limited mortal nature is key to healing, as well as understanding why we desire to hide from our emotions. Our mortal nature sometimes feels foreign to our spiritual selves. For that reason, we tend to ignore our mortal feelings or try to hide them.

In addition to being unable to effectively express our emotions because of past hurts, we live in a society that has taught us expressing feelings is a sign of weakness. It's a highly individualistic society where we're told to be strong and tough and that crying is weak, especially for our male population.[10] As mentioned before, this is this isn't true. It takes strength to show vulnerability in the expression of our emotions. Only strong people can accept when they are hurting. Our emotions exist for a reason.

However, our society is learning the importance of expressing feelings and their significance in overall emotional and physical health.[11] A helpful visual I use with my clients to demonstrate our ability and willingness to know our emotional self comes through Mother Earth. Because of our acculturation and biological limitations and hidden emotional pain, especially during our childhood years, I equate us to Mother Earth; she has a hard rock shell and active magma at her core.

This magma is what makes her alive. It creates new land and contributes to the oxygen we breathe. We also have a core of emotions and feelings that make us alive and contribute to our daily growth. The active ones are beautiful and they make life exciting and worth living. For example, the joy we feel playing with a child or holding a newborn baby. These are active feelings, which can lead to great joy and happiness.

We, like Mother Earth, also have a hard shell. This shell is formed after years of burying unresolved pain and emotions. All of our thoughts and actions are fueled by these active and inactive repressed emotions. If we're acting, there is a feeling and a thought behind it. Sometimes we don't understand or know what those feelings and thoughts are because they are buried too deep, being too painful.

We have feelings first, which then lead to thoughts and afterward to actions.

When we don't like what we're feeling or thinking (mostly due to the pain), I have seen individuals cover it with some form of addiction. I've seen people with drug and alcohol addiction, work addiction, religious addiction, shopping addiction, recreation addiction, pornography and sex addiction, bulimia, anorexia, overeating, and self-harm to name a few.

At the point of addiction or addictive tendencies, I have seen my clients become more susceptible to feelings of guilt, anxiety, depression, and hopelessness. It becomes a cycle that can be difficult to break, but not impossible.

Awareness is key. We can't change anything we aren't aware of. To heal from buried pain and overcome our desire to hide from it, we need to metaphorically take a chisel and hammer and break up our hard shell so it can bubble up to the surface where we can see it and be aware of it.

It's imperative for us to feel the pain behind these emotions and feelings in order to heal. This pain affects everything we do in our lives. Karol Kuhn Truman once wrote a book called *Feelings Buried Alive Never Die*, which describes how these buried emotions affect us physically in our everyday activities. It is a great reference book to see what emotions we have hidden and how they display themselves. We have to feel to heal, and then we can feel the peace and comfort that we all desire and deserve.

Mother Earth can also teach us additional lessons about our feelings and emotions and healthy ways of handling them. When Mother Earth develops too much pressure from this hot, bubbling magma, she releases the pressure by bringing it to the surface and blowing it out through a volcano. These volcanoes are destructive in nature and sometimes cause irreversible damage. This is exactly what happens with us when we build up too much pressure from our emotions. We blow up like a volcano. Our volcanoes are similarly destructive and sometimes cause irreversible damage. When we explode with inappropriate anger, effective communication cannot happen. These explosions actually contribute to the destruction of relationships.

I counsel many married couples who use inappropriate anger to try and communicate something that is important to them. I'll never forget one young couple who told me of a fight where harsh words were used and resulted in them not speaking with each other for days unless absolutely necessary. After figuring out that this behavior was ineffective and didn't get the result she wanted, one day the wife sat calmly and listened to the husband as he yelled that she was not home enough, that she needed to take their marriage more seriously and perform her so-called duties, which required her to be home more, not out with her friends.

The wife listened to him vent, and because she was only listening and not engaging in the drama of the moment, the husband eventually calmed down. When he did, the wife asked him lovingly what was wrong. He got tears in his eyes and said, "Why don't you ever want to be with me?" The husband was able to express what he was truly feeling. He was feeling rejection, not anger, and because he communicated his true feelings, the couple then had the tools to make an effective plan for the future.

The ironic part is we tend to release the most anger with those whom we love and trust. It is because of this trust that we feel safe enough to vent. We believe that our families and those we love will accept us no matter what. However, when we frequently release emotion in an unhealthy, dysfunctional manner, it becomes habitual and generational in nature. Children learn what they live, which makes it difficult, though not impossible, to unlearn the dysfunction and replace it with healthy and appropriate ways of releasing our emotions.

Again we can learn from Mother Earth about healthy ways of releasing our steam. One of her most effective and healthy releases is called Yellowstone National Park. Yellowstone is constantly releasing steam. She has little geysers, big geysers, mud pots, and steaming pools. We need to create and develop a Yellowstone in our lives if we want to release and manage our emotional pressure effectively. Some of these emotional releases could be regular exercise, journaling, artistic and musical expression, prayer, reading scriptures or other enjoyable books, or just plain shouting to the top of our lungs (only when other people are not around). But, remember, it is important for your Yellowstone to be personalized for you. If it's going to work for you, it needs to come from you.

As previously stated, all through childhood we experience at least intermittent pain. Most of this pain is forced down to a place where it becomes hard to identify. Everything that happened in childhood affects our lives as adults. We live with this inadequate ability to reason for so long that the dysfunctional thoughts and emotions that occur become an ingrained part of our daily functioning and reality. Guilt, shame, and inadequacy often become prevalent residual feelings. Guilt and shame become Lucifer's playground until we learn the skills to manage our emotions and heal from our painful pasts. How do we keep our control and not allow Lucifer to have any power over us? How do we heal so we can feel the peace Christ intended for us instead of the turmoil Lucifer desires to magnify?

Awareness and willingness to feel is the first step toward healthy, functional healing. Christ taught us when He was on earth that we have the ability to heal through His light if we have enough faith. Faith is positive energy directed toward Christ. All positive energy comes through Christ. All healing comes through Christ. Everything good comes through Christ.

2

Releasing Guilt and Becoming as a Little Child

So here we are, adults, survivors of childhood, carrying a lot of guilt and pain until we heal. We've been taught that we are to become as a little child to enter into the kingdom of heaven (see Matthew 18:3). What does that journey look like? Surviving childhood, becoming adults, and then becoming as a little child again?

Have you ever wondered what it means to "become as a little child"? What would we need to feel? What would our behaviors be like? Our attitudes? What would we be thinking and doing? What would our goals be?

This task, becoming as a little child, has a lot to do with the difference between guilt and remorse. What is the difference between guilt and remorse? For one, they are at opposite ends of the spectrum, in the same way that happiness and sadness are opposites, black and white, hot and cold. But remorse and guilt are more aligned on the spectrum of light and darkness or evil and righteousness, with remorse being on the righteous or light side and guilt being on the evil or dark side.

To understand this point, it's important to emphasize that the Lord is bound by universal laws, one being justice and another being opposition in all things. As we know, we needed the Savior to satisfy justice for us because of our mortal natures. We all needed the Savior's mercy because we could not satisfy the law of justice on our own. With opposition in all things, Satan followed the Lord's plan when he approached Eve with the forbidden fruit, tempting her into partaking of it, thus creating the dark side of the spectrum. If there's light, there must also be darkness.

Guilt is negative or dark energy and remorse is positive or light energy. Remorse is part of the remarkable process of forgiveness, part of the path back to our Heavenly Father. The only way we can enter into the kingdom of heaven is through the repentance process and becoming as a little child. There must be a correlation, and I believe it has to do with feelings of remorse, which are a key step in repenting.

How can we know and feel the difference between feelings of guilt and remorse? Godly sorrow is remorse and worldly sorrow is guilt, as taught by President Uchtdorf:

> There is an important difference between the sorrow for sin that leads to repentance and the sorrow that leads to despair. The Apostle Paul taught that "*godly sorrow* worketh repentance to salvation . . . but the *sorrow of the world* worketh death." *Godly sorrow* inspires change and hope through the Atonement of Jesus Christ. *Worldly sorrow* pulls us down, extinguishes hope, and persuades us to give in to further temptation. *Godly sorrow* leads to conversion and a change of heart. It causes us to hate sin and love goodness. It encourages us to stand up and walk in the light of Christ's love. . . . But when guilt leads to self-loathing or prevents us from rising up again, it is impeding rather than promoting our repentance.[1]

Of course we don't like it when we make mistakes. It feels awful. Satan is highly aware of the difference between worldly sorrow and godly sorrow and how worldly sorrow beats us down, making us believe we need to be different than who we are. President Uchtdorf continues with this point by stating, "One of the adversary's methods to prevent us from progressing is to confuse us about who we really are and what we really desire."[2]

Satan's goal is our destruction. The Lord's goal is our growth through the positive process of repentance. Guilt is worldly sorrow and remorse is godly sorrow. The outcomes of these two feelings are opposite: one leads to growth and light while the other leads to death and destruction. Guilt turns the focus back on us as the individual, as if we could be different than who we are and somehow have the ability to fix ourselves, which we don't and never will. Remorse turns the focus to Christ where it belongs.

The Parable of the Mud Field

To explain this difference further, let's again imagine when we came to earth, we were all placed in a mud field where we are to journey through the muck until we come to the edge and are rescued, washed off, and placed in a beautiful garden through the process of Christ's Atonement and the miracle of the resurrection. We were all dumped into the mud field. No one can escape from the certain and everlasting death without Christ's atoning sacrifice. We will all be rescued from the mud field even if we don't move an inch toward the garden afterward because Christ saved all men through His sacrifice.

I see our earth life as falling into this huge field of mud. We're here in the mud during our whole mortal existence. It's up to us to keep moving through the mud, utilizing the process of repentance and looking toward Christ in every action and deed. Following Christ and looking toward Him constantly is the only way to keep moving through the mud. Otherwise we become stuck, unable to move further. We might even begin to sink unless we focus on Christ and the garden. If we keep our eyes on Christ, we continually move toward a beautiful garden on the other side of the mud field, a garden full of flowers, fruits, vegetables, perfect temperatures, and people we love. Most important, Christ is there waiting for us to come to Him so He can welcome us into His garden with loving arms.

Our goal is to get across this muddy field to reach the promised state of happiness and security. We're only strong enough to do it if we keep looking toward Christ, who is directing us on how to get through. Without His direction, we become lost and can't see clearly. Our job is simple: we need to take one step and then another toward the garden, enduring and always focusing on the garden, never doubting, never fearing, never slowing down enough to begin sinking.

We need to recognize that we *are on a journey* through the mud and we are all dirty throughout the trek. Many others are also trekking through the mud alongside us. Not one of them is clean. Not one of them is better than the other. At any given moment, if we stop and lose direction, each one of us has the possibility of sinking or becoming stuck. We only become clean when Christ washes us off. The layers of filth are only gone as Christ bathes us with His sacrifice and love.

The Fallen Man

We must understand our complete dependence on Christ for us to enter into the kingdom of heaven. Just as a child is utterly dependent on their parents for survival, we are also utterly dependent on Christ for our survival and rescue from the filth of the mud field. So to become like a little child, we need to *accept* the limitations of being mortal here on earth in the mud with no escape, except through Christ. Accepting our limitations is key. It's the difference between becoming as a little child and following his or her rescuer with gratitude, or being prideful, believing we could or should be able to save ourselves. We can't, and we will never be able to.

Our journey was deliberately designed by a loving Heavenly Father. He knew that if He let us make the journey through the field, we would learn to be independent, gain experience in life, and be better people in the end. So we came here and fell into the mud. There is nothing we could ever do to change this fact. We are dirty and have been dirty during our whole existence here on earth. In the Book of Mormon, it states that "because of the fall our natures have become evil continually" (Ether 3:2).

Everything we do that is righteous and uplifting here on earth is through the power of Christ. The Book of Mormon prophet Jacob gave great insight into our natural disposition and the state of our existence without the Atonement.

> Our spirits must become subject to that angel who fell from before
> the presence of the Eternal God, and became the devil, to rise no

more. And our spirits *must* have become like unto him, and we become devils, angels to a devil, to be shut out from the presence of our God, and to remain with the father of lies, in misery, like unto himself . . . O how great the goodness of our God, who prepareth a way for our escape from the grasp of this awful monster. (2 Nephi 9:8–10; italics added)

What a harrowing thought, that without Jesus we would become like unto the devil himself! And what rejoicing we can have at the goodness and mercy of our Heavenly Father and Jesus, who prepared a way for us to overcome this condition. The essential factor in deciding our fate starts with awareness of who we are and how we became that way, accepting it, and then making our choice of who we are going to follow each day. We cannot in any way overcome this condition on our own.

Let's look at how a child might feel about being rescued from the mud field in comparison to how an adult would feel. A young child being rescued would be tired, hungry, and cold, but extremely grateful for being rescued from almost certain death. He sees his rescuer as a hero, one he might like to emulate and follow. He rejoices in the weeks to come when he sees the man who saved him. He might run with all his might to get his savior's attention and to ask him if there is anything he might be able to do to help him. The young child always remembers the man who saved him and tries to become like him as he grows up, helping other people along the way. He runs to greet him and hug him whenever he sees him to thank him again. He has found a true friend and mentor. The child learns to love even more as he tries to serve him and be like him.

Now, a grown man being rescued would feel tired, hungry, and cold as the little child did and also extremely grateful for his rescue. But the difference comes as, because of our human natures, the man might feel embarrassed or ashamed that he wasn't looking where he was going or taking the appropriate measures to keep himself from becoming stuck. He might feel upset that so much manpower was required to save him, to pull him from the mud. He might start to feel guilty that his rescue took someone's time when his rescuer should have been focusing on and taking care of his own problems and concerns. The man might feel upset that he couldn't find a way to save himself from the mud. He might even feel embarrassed enough to go out of his way to avoid his rescuer when he sees him down the road. He might feel awful that he had to be saved from the mud, taking someone else's time and talents when they did not do anything to deserve getting dirty by rescuing him. Often, we tend to embrace guilt instead of remorse because we don't like to recognize the feeling that we needed to be rescued and saved. We don't recognize our limitations or we are unwilling to accept them.

Many of us struggle with this issue, and Lucifer *loves* it because we then feel guilty for being who we are! This has become one of his favorite traps because how could we be any different than who we are? When we cannot, or will not, accept the ugly aspects of our mortality, we don't have the ability to take control, manage, or overcome our mortality the way that Christ has taught us to do.

The Difference between Guilt and Remorse

The difference between guilt and remorse shown in the example above is how the man feels guilty for his limitations. His guilt stems from the fact that he cannot save himself. He feels that he should be able to save himself. The child does not. The child accepts his limitations and is simply grateful for the rescue.

This difference is huge. This difference between guilt, which is Lucifer's tool, and remorse, which is Heavenly Father's tool, is important to recognize, understand, and differentiate. Guilt turns the focus back on us as the individual. Remorse turns the focus to Christ where it belongs. He already did the work for us, and if we focus on guilt, it's like saying to Him, "I'll take care of this myself." Recognizing what He went through for us individually and collectively, can we keep saying this to Him?

Many, if not all, of us fall into Lucifer's web of guilt. It's easy to do because guilt is what could be called a half-truth. Lucifer loves to use half-truths because there's some measure of truth in them, so we're more easily swayed into believing the lie as if it were truth. Guilt is a half-truth because we are supposed to feel bad when we have done something wrong. However, the outcome of guilt focuses on us, the individual, when it should be on Christ.

Another difference is that remorse is productive whereas guilt is not. Guilt is like sitting in a rocking chair when you are trying to travel across the country. It doesn't take us anywhere. It's self-defeating, self-degrading. This is the main reason the adversary loves to use it. Guilt has the potential of pulling or driving us down into a pit of despair that becomes difficult to climb back out of once inside. Guilt focuses on us in a negative and destructive way, derailing our energies that could be put toward productive goals and objectives.

On the other hand, remorse places the focus into the productive and healthy process of healing. Remorse is part of the remarkable and productive process of repentance. It's an action word. When we have done something requiring forgiveness, remorse is there to help us achieve this goal. It contains a broken heart and contrite spirit (see 3 Nephi 9:20): a broken heart because we're broken-hearted that Jesus suffered for us and a contrite spirit because we know we have to accept His suffering to overcome our problems. We recognize there is no other way to succeed. Heavenly Father uses remorse to build us back up from our shortcomings. We can use remorse as a tool to forgive ourselves for our mistakes. Most significantly, remorse gives us the understanding that we can't fix ourselves. Christ has already paid for our sins, so we don't have to spend time trying to pay for something that's already been bought for us, something we could never do in the first place.

When we reach a point of understanding, clarity, and feel gratitude for our salvation, we can decide to follow Christ in every thought and deed. It then becomes possible for us to forgive ourselves of past mistakes. We can move forward, step by step, in a healthy manner toward our goal of eternal life in our Heavenly Father's presence.

Nephi described in depth how he struggled with his mortality and his mistakes:

> Behold, my soul delighteth in the things of the Lord; and my heart pondereth continually upon the things which I have seen and heard. Nevertheless, notwithstanding the great goodness of the Lord, in showing me His great and marvelous works, my heart exclaimeth: O wretched man that I am! Yea, my heart sorroweth because of my flesh; my soul grieveth because of mine iniquities. I am encompassed

about, because of the temptations and the sins which do so easily
beset me. And when I desire to rejoice, my heart groaneth because
of my sins; nevertheless, I know in whom I have trusted. . . . O then,
if I have seen so great things, if the Lord in his condescension unto
the children of men hath visited men in so much mercy, why should
my heart weep and my soul linger in the valley of sorrow, and my
flesh waste away, and my strength slacken, because of mine afflictions?
And why should I yield to sin, because of my flesh? Yea, why should
I give way to temptations, that the evil one have place in my heart
to destroy my peace and afflict my soul? Why am I angry because of
mine enemy? Awake, my soul! No longer droop in sin. Rejoice, O my
heart, and give place no more for the enemy of my soul. Do not anger
again because of mine enemies. Do not slacken my strength because
of mine afflictions. Rejoice, O my heart, and cry unto the Lord, and
say: O Lord, I will praise thee forever; yea, my soul will rejoice in thee,
my God, and the rock of my salvation. O Lord, wilt thou redeem my
soul? Wilt thou deliver me out of the hands of mine enemies? Wilt
thou make me that I may shake at the appearance of sin? (2 Nephi
4:16–19, 26–31)

The Apostle Paul also described his individual struggle in a similar manner:

For we know that the law is spiritual: but I am carnal, sold under sin.
. . . But I see another law in my members, warring against the law of
my mind, and bringing me into captivity to the law of sin which is in
my members. O wretched man that I am! Who shall deliver me from
the body of this death? I thank God through Jesus Christ our Lord.
So then with the mind I myself serve the law of God; but with the
flesh the law of sin. (Romans 7:14, 23–25)

In these excerpts, both Nephi and Paul recognized their mortality.
They recognized they were fallen men. They did not enjoy the feelings they were both having about their limitations and their inability
to save themselves. But they also understood that the only way to
be delivered from their mortal bondage is through the atoning sacrifice of Christ and by following His teachings. They changed the
guilt they were feeling to remorse as they turned to Christ for relief
and accepted his gift, the gift of His Atonement. These great men

demonstrate a common struggle of humanity. They worked through their mortality and turned to Christ with feelings of remorse and gratitude for their rescue and their chance to return to Heavenly Father.

A distinct difference exists between the godly sorrow that worketh repentance (see 2 Corinthians 7:10), which involves personal suffering, and the easy, relatively painless sorrow for being caught. Mormon described this misplaced sorrow as "the sorrowing of the damned, because the Lord would not always suffer them to take happiness in sin" (Mormon 2:13).

We don't have the tools or ability to save ourselves due to our mortal natures. It's vital to look at our condition and our situation realistically and clearly. This is the first step in change and growth. After our assessment, we can make goals toward our growth to become like the Savior. Our role here on earth includes recognition and acceptance that we're either going to keep moving or we're going to sink. That is what enduring to the end means: that we need to keep moving toward Christ, keeping our eyes and focus on Him. "Look unto me in every thought; doubt not, fear not" (D&C 6:36). Christ is the source of all light in this world. He is the root of everything good. Even thermodynamic scientists, who study light and heat, have said that when something is removed from its source of light and energy, it will become disorganized, ultimately losing its energy and becoming dark. This is one of the laws of thermodynamics.[3] As all things typify Christ, the same process happens with us. If we are constantly moving toward the source of all light and energy, accepting His role in our salvation and obeying His commandments to the best of our ability, then we are "held together" by being close to that light. Once we remove ourselves from Christ by any means, including focusing on our own guilty feelings, we begin to fall apart and lose our energy and light.

I've seen so many examples that illustrate how easy it is to sink under guilt's negative power, stories from my previous clients who became emotionally and even somewhat physically paralyzed with guilt. It actually controlled almost everything they did every day.

Imagine a woman who accidentally hit and killed a young child with her car as he was crossing the street, running after a ball. This woman would likely feel severe guilt from this accident. If the guilt becomes bad enough, she could believe she doesn't deserve to live. Every time she might feel any joy or happiness, or catch herself laughing, she immediately stops herself, believing she doesn't deserve to feel anything good ever again. She knows how devastated she'd feel to lose one of her own children, and she can't resolve her feelings toward herself for causing someone else, another mother, that level of pain.

I've known people who have been severely sexually abused, sometimes by even friends or family members. This kind of horrific abuse can continue for years. From my experience counseling these victims, they become afraid of divulging the abuse. Guilt often consumes the victim's faith and motivation because they believe that it's somehow their fault, that they must have done something wrong to deserve the abuse.

Both of these examples are extreme, but they illustrate how guilt can destroy our lives, effectively paralyzing us, stopping our progression and placing us at risk of sinking in the mud. Those involved in these examples would place the blame on themselves for the negative events that occurred in their lives. That is exactly what guilt does. What we don't recognize is that blame implies intent, and neither intended for such awful things to happen.

The woman did not intend to hit the young boy and sexually abused victims did not intend to be abused. So, with these two examples, guilt and blame should not be a part of their journey in the mud. Situations like these become Lucifer's hunting grounds. He utilizes some of his greatest power to destroy self-worth in circumstances like these. He understands we would naturally feel horrible about them and he manipulates the emotional response we experience, planting half-truths in our minds until we believe them in our hearts.

By allowing Lucifer to control our emotions, our heavenward progression stops, which inhibits our ability to accomplish what the Lord would have us do. In principle, faith and fear (or guilt) cannot reside in a person at the same time because they are opposite emotions that therefore create opposite outcomes (see 2 Timothy 1:7, Mosiah 7:12–19, *Lectures on Faith*, third lecture, paragraphs 19–21.)

As mentioned before, fear and guilt focus on us individually, para-lyzing our growth. Faith is the exact the opposite, creating a differ-ent outcome when it is coupled with remorse. It is when we utilize faith and remorse that we can turn toward our Savior for the relief and development that is necessary in our individual circumstances. Lucifer can manipulate all of us if we allow him, though this control and manipulation is directly piloted, in varying degrees, by our own actions and beliefs.

Richard G. Scott stated, in his talk entitled "To Heal the Shat-tering Consequences of Abuse," that

> if you have been abused, Satan will strive to convince you that there is no solution. Yet he knows perfectly well that there is. Satan recog-nizes that healing comes through the unwavering love of Heavenly Father for each of His children. He also understands that the power of healing is inherent in the Atonement of Jesus Christ. Therefore, his strategy is to do all possible to separate you from your Father and His Son. Do not let Satan convince you that you are beyond help. Satan uses your abuse to undermine your self-confidence, destroy trust in authority, create fear, and generate feelings of despair. . . . While these outcomes have powerful influence in your life, *they do not define the real you.*[4]

When we have sinned, Satan tries to convince us that there aren't any solutions. President Kimball so beautifully explains in the fol-lowing statement how, when we've sinned, there is always forgive-ness available. We can never sin too much: "Sometimes . . . when a repentant one looks back and sees the ugliness, the loathsomeness of the transgression, he is almost overwhelmed and wonders, 'Can the Lord ever forgive me? Can I ever forgive myself?' But when one reaches the depths of despondency and feels the hopelessness of his position, and when he cries out to God for mercy in helplessness but in faith, there comes a still, small, but penetrating voice whispering to his soul, 'Thy sins are forgiven thee.'"[5]

We have all been given the opportunity to come to earth and obtain a mortal body that we know is evil and carnal in nature. This mortal being feels different or maybe even foreign to our heavenly spirit that united with it as our spirits came directly from a perfect lineage: our heavenly parents. Heavenly Father understands this challenge given to us and accepts and loves us for who we are no matter what mistakes we make while here on earth. He is our only source of eternal love during our earthly existence.

The Pure Love of Christ

The Lord will never turn us away if we turn to Him in repentance (see Helaman 13:11). It is near impossible to lose His acceptance, His help, or His love. This is a difficult concept for many to accept and understand because the world we live in is conditional. Contracts and promises can be broken, and people can be mistrustful or resentful. Everything here on earth is transient, each one of us, with our imperfect mortal dispositions. In contrast, Christ's love and acceptance are not; He is ready to forgive us repeatedly.

I have always desired to be loved eternally. I know I'm not unique in this desire because I see this with a number of my clients. The problem many run into is we are looking for this eternal love in the wrong places. We might be looking for it with our partners, our children and grandchildren, friends, or addictions. The list goes on. We will never find eternal love if we don't look for it at its source. The only source of this eternal love here on earth is through our Savior, Jesus Christ.

Many might think this idea is wrong, that they do love their children or spouse eternally. But we don't. We're mortals, meaning we're conditional. The closest feeling to eternal love on earth is the love parents have for a child, but even then we are still transient beings. This is difficult for parents to process. I used to believe and hope that I loved all of my sons eternally, the way Heavenly Father does, but if one of them tried to harm me, he would no longer be allowed in my presence. I would want to continue loving him no matter what his behaviors, but in my imperfect mortal state, my feelings would change if the behaviors continued. I know that I could not allow the behaviors.

Loving someone is different from not loving his or her behaviors. I can still love my children even if their behaviors are unacceptable sometimes. As mortals, we can accept only so much, even from our children. Mortals have limits.

Remember, we can practically do nothing here that will ever turn Christ away from us as long as we are still seeking Him. Each week, as we attend our church services and partake of the sacrament, the Lord forgives us. Every week we renew our covenants to follow Him by taking the sacrament. He is always eager and willing to help us, and we only have to accept it.

I worked for two years with a number of felons who desperately verbalized a desire to change their lives for the better. They were accepted into a program where it became their last chance to prove themselves before they went away to prison for a long time. Many of them had lost the support of their family members because their actions had been too hurtful for too long. The felons approached their family members, explaining the nature of the program and asking for their help, with what I perceived to be a high level of humility and sorrow, but the family members were still guarded. They'd heard too many stories or promises of change before. This is the conditional nature of our mortality.

Christ will never turn us away no matter how many times we have disappointed Him or continue to do the same wrong over and over again. Spencer W. Kimball explained, "Jesus saw sin as wrong but also was able to see sin as springing from deep and unmet needs on the part of the sinner. This permitted Him to condemn the sin without condemning the individual."[6] Therefore, because of His willingness to be ever present, He becomes the only source of eternal love, as long as we look toward Him while moving forward through the mud field. That is why He is our Savior. He is always there to help us, to save us, to redeem us.

As I said earlier, in our journey through the mud field, our assignment is simple. All we have to do is look continually toward the garden while we are trudging through the mud, making mistake after mistake but repenting along the way. No matter how many of those mistakes we make, if we are still trudging through the mud, looking toward Christ, He will never turn us away when we approach Him.

One of Christ's apostle's, Peter, was able to walk on water as long as his faith was focused on Christ (see Matthew 14:29–31). But the moment Peter let fear replace his faith, he looked away and sunk into the water. Christ immediately reached His hand toward Peter and pulled him out. Peter focused on Christ again and was able to walk on water along with Christ, and the wind subsided as they reached the boat.

Christ was teaching Peter an important life lesson for reaching his goal of returning to Heavenly Father. Christ taught Peter that though he might fall, the Savior would always be there to extend His hand and pull him back on track. As long as we look toward Christ, we're able to keep moving. When we lose our focus, we can get stuck and start to sink.

Jesus Christ, with His infinite Atonement, is the source of all light and goodness. Elder Cook said, "Freedom and light have never been easy to attain or maintain. Since the War in Heaven, the forces of evil have used every means possible to destroy agency and extinguish light."[7] Lucifer is actively utilizing his best and most durable tools to destroy all light here on earth. Guilt is a favorite tool because it works well with all of his lies and half-truths, of which guilt is one.

We can keep our light and have peace and joy. We need to look to Christ, from whom all light comes. "And that which doth not edify is not of God, and is darkness. That which is of God is light; and he that receiveth light, and continueth in God, receiveth more light; and that light groweth brighter and brighter until the perfect day" (D&C 50:23–24).

Moroni excellently explains how all light and goodness comes through Christ in the following verses:

> Wherefore, all things which are good cometh of God; and that which is evil cometh of the devil; for the devil is an enemy unto God, and fighteth against Him continually, and inviteth and enticeth to sin, and to do that which is evil continually. . . . Wherefore, take heed, my beloved brethren, that ye do not judge that which is evil to be of God, or that which is good and of God to be of the devil. . . . For behold, the Spirit of Christ is given to every man, that he may know good from evil; wherefore, I show unto you the way to judge; for every thing which inviteth to do good, and to persuade to believe in Christ, is sent forth by the power and gift of Christ; wherefore ye may know with a perfect knowledge it is of God. But whatsoever thing persuadeth men to do evil, and believe not in Christ, and deny Him, and serve not God, then ye may know with a perfect knowledge it is

of the devil; for after this manner doth the devil work, for he persua-
deth no man to do good, no, not one; neither do his angels; neither
do they who subject themselves unto him. (Moroni 7:12, 14, 16–17)

Again, all light and goodness comes from Christ, and all people
are blessed with the His Spirit. All are able to judge good from evil
because of the gift of the Spirit of Christ. Positive self-esteem and
self-worth are part of the goodness and light that comes through
Christ. Anything that destroys self-worth and self-esteem is then, of
course, from the adversary. This targeted effort to destroy our worth
individually and collectively as a society, nation, and world by Satan
is in opposition of the Lord's plan and desire for us.

It's imperative to emphasize again that the Lord is bound by universal laws. One of those laws is justice. For this reason, we needed
a Savior to satisfy that law. Another one of the laws is opposition in
all things. Because of this law, there will always be two clear ends
of the spectrum. It's essential for us to be aware of both ends of
the spectrum, and for us to see clearly the ends for the purpose of
differentiating them. For example, if we can't clearly see black and
white, we are less able to understand the gray. So awareness is essential. Awareness provides understanding and clarity of where we are
and where we are headed. Darkness and light are the two ends of the
spectrum universally. The adversary brings darkness and evil into the
world whereas the Lord brings light and goodness.

Guilt is on the dark end of the spectrum, the adversary's side. It
effectively destroys our self-worth by placing the focus and responsibility of being perfect on us. How could guilt not make us feel horrible when it constantly berates us for not being able to be different
than who we are?

Remorse, on the other hand, is on the Lord's end of the spectrum. Remorse helps us to grow and understand our weaknesses and
inabilities. Remorse helps us to understand the state of our imperfect
mortal natures. It helps us to grow emotionally and spiritually by
allowing Christ to be our Savior, allows us feelings of gratitude for
His atoning, eternal sacrifice, and helps us to want to be like Christ.
When we understand our failing and inability to save ourselves, only
then can we move forward and grow emotionally and spiritually,

accepting Christ in our lives. To accept Him in our lives, we have to accept what He did for us and we have to follow His example through daily thoughts and actions.

Christ wants us to follow His example. Guilt gets us stuck in the mud. Remorse keeps us moving through it, fueled by feelings of gratitude.

Two opposite ends of the spectrum: light and darkness. Remorse and guilt.

3

Two Powerful Words

Understanding who we are is crucial in order to combat the adversary. Satan knows the power of healthy self-worth and self-esteem so he is working to destroy recognition of our divine nature and abilities. He realizes that a sense of divine worth can bring a high level of peace and happiness, which can lead to successful, healthy relationships and behaviors.

The adversary recognizes this inherent weakness in us and targets our self-worth. Lucifer uses his powerful tools, like guilt, to accomplish his desires of destroying our self-worth and the possibility of our eternal salvation.

Elder Cook explained, "An ever-present danger to the family is the onslaught of evil forces that seem to come from every direction. . . . These evil forces remove light and hope from the world. The level of decadence is accelerating. If we do not black out evil from our homes and lives, do not be surprised if devastating moral explosions shatter the peace which is the reward for righteous living. Our responsibility is to be in the world but not of the world."[1]

Lucifer is in full force, trying to destroy our family units and our individual salvation. He uses multiple tools to harm many of our young men's self-worth. Most young men I have counseled have an incredibly strong desire to live a righteous, Christ-centered life. But many of them struggle with pornography and other related vices and the associated guilt because of their actions.

They make progress toward a goal of abstinence often because of their desire to overcome it. They implement safety plans such as controlling Internet and television access. But even with safety measures in place, these young men continue to struggle with their problems every day. And they often report that they emotionally beat themselves up with guilt. It becomes a whirlpool of destruction with the possibility of pulling them down further into a pit of despair and self-degradation. The struggle these young man feel is not unique.

Lucifer knows the power of his most useful tools. He wants us to feel guilt and turmoil on a constant basis just because of who we are. Our focus becomes trying to change who we are instead of accepting it and learning to manage our natures.

When we are fighting against who we are rather than accepting it, we start to feel destructive feelings inside. And when that happens it's like metaphorically clenching our fists constantly. The relentless clenching requires real energy—it makes us tired and we start to feel defeated or too tired to accomplish healthy and functional objectives, ones that lead toward our intended missions here on earth. It's difficult to do any tasks if our fists are clenched.

To let go of the guilt we feel and regain our strength, we need to accept the reality of it and be aware of where it is coming from. Lucifer loves it when we feel guilt and turmoil for something we can't change. One of those things we cannot change is the fact that we have carnal or mortal natures. It's all right that we have these natures because it's part of our mortal experience. There is nothing wrong or sinful with having mortal, human natures, but God's commandments do instruct us on how to use our natures to become more like Him. This acceptance of a carnal nature is a difficult concept for a lot of people to embrace. Many of us try to change this condition, but we can't. When we can't change this fact but we want to, Lucifer uses guilt like a hammer to pound away until we take it out of his hands and we proceed to pound ourselves with our own guilt.

He wants us to feel guilt and turmoil continually. He knows that if we have knowledge and understanding of what is behind the negative energy, we can obtain some level of control and let go of the toxicity. Instead of turmoil and uneasiness inside, the result is the peace that Christ intended us to feel. Finding this peace does require effort and faith on our part. Christ wants us to feel the peace of knowing He already saved us from certain death and is always with us, ready and willing to help and comfort us when we need Him.

One of the hardest things to do in life is accept the reality of our natures. We tend to resist this and fight it at every level. But we need to accept our inability to fix our natures on our own merits and instead look toward Christ in every thought and deed (see D&C 6:36) to help us overcome our natures.

Resisting our natures is difficult to do in our instant-gratification society. However, we manage our mortal natures if we desire to find true happiness and joy in life. If you think about what it means to be a *disciple* of Christ, it really comes down to being *disciplined* in our faith and humility to follow God's commandments. Christ knows we're all imperfect. He understands our limited capacities while in our mortal state. Christ doesn't want us to ever feel guilty because of our mortal condition. He wants us to accept it and turn to Him for growth and light to ultimately overcome our condition in the end.

So it is possible to feel peace. As mentioned previously, one of the reasons for our inability to feel peace is that we continue to reflect upon past mistakes and continue to make additional mistakes. It's not easy to resolve our inappropriate past actions in our minds and hearts if we do not realize that making mistakes is part of life. Only the infinite and eternal sacrifice of Jesus Christ can reconcile the gap, and this is something we must come to understand.

Accepting our inability to overcome mortality is a step toward healing and finding strength through our Savior, Jesus Christ. His infinite and eternal sacrifice is the only way to overcome our mistakes. In the Book of Mormon, the prophet Alma described how he was overwhelmed with guilt after he had committed so many sins, to the point that he believed he could not be forgiven.

> Yea, I did remember all my sins and iniquities, for which I was tormented with the pains of hell; yea, I saw that I had rebelled against my God, and that I had not kept His holy commandments. . . . And

it came to pass that as I was thus racked with torment, while I was harrowed up by the memory of my many sins, behold, I remembered . . . the coming of one Jesus Christ, a Son of God, to atone for the sins of the world. Now, as my mind caught hold upon this thought, I cried within my heart: O Jesus, thou Son of God, have mercy on me, who am in the gall of bitterness, and am encircled about by the everlasting chains of death. And now, behold, when I thought this, I could remember my pains no more; yea, I was harrowed up by the memory of my sins no more. And oh, what joy, and what marvelous light I did behold; yea, my soul was filled with joy as exceeding as was my pain! (Alma 36:13, 17–20)

By accepting our state as imperfect beings that make mistakes, and looking to our Savior's infinite and eternal sacrifice, we can experience the same results that Alma experienced. When Alma accepted and cried out to the Lord for help, he was filled with joy and peace. He accepted his shortcomings and didn't focus on blaming himself. When the blame is gone, it's possible for us to feel more peace and forgiveness toward ourselves and others.

We have been promised that we will remember our pains and sins no more. Instead of guilty feelings, we will be filled with joy and marvelous light as great as any feelings of pain we ever experienced. The possibility of accomplishing the Lord's goals for Him becomes much greater when there is peace.

To help us start this process we need to remember two powerful words: I Am.

I Am means God, as spoken of in the Holy Bible (see Exodus 3:14). It also represents our ability to accept ourselves as we are, which is often something different than how we hope to be seen. Until we accept ourselves entirely—with all our strengths but also all our weaknesses, all the good and all the bad, all our beauty but also our ugliness, our capacity to love but also our capacity to hate—we will not be able to grow as we should.

We are unable to change anything we are not aware of. Awareness is the critical part of change, with acceptance being the next. If we make the effort to understand ourselves as we truly are, it will free us from the limitations we all create when we are only picking and choosing our best parts to show the world. By accepting our elemental self, we will know the truth and it will make us free (see John 8:32).

I Am means God, and it also means accepting ourselves as we truly are. By writing or stating these two words while thinking of the meaning behind them, we can accept our mortality with all of its faults and also accept that we are good enough to partake of Jesus Christ's infinite Atonement. By believing in ourselves and realizing we are divine and precious beings, we take the first steps toward healing and automatically become beings that can perform miracles. Or more specifically, we become beings in whom the miracle of the Atonement is performed and we are filled with joy and light beyond comprehension.

Just as awareness of ourselves is essential to overcome our own weaknesses, awareness of Lucifer and his tactics is also essential. We can take back control and focus on our goal of following Christ and His teachings.

Elder Bednar explained the importance of awareness as we battle our enemies.

Because today we are engaged in a war for the welfare of marriage and the home, in my latest reading of the Book of Mormon I paid particular attention to the ways the Nephites prepared for their battles against the Lamanites. I noted that the people of Nephi "were *aware of the intent* of [their enemy], and therefore they did prepare to meet them" (Alma 2:12; italics added). As I read and studied, I learned that *understanding the intent of an enemy* is a key prerequisite to effective preparation. We likewise should consider the intent of our enemy in this latter-day war.[2]

Book Two: Knowing Our Common Enemy

4

Lucifer's Unique Toolbox

Can you imagine being in a marriage where you've lost your memory completely? You have a spouse and children, but you don't remember any of them. It would take a lot of faith and trust to believe what's told to you about who you are, where you belong, and what you do in your life. You would have to rely on glimpses of memory or feelings you might have when familiar and comfortable moments come.

Guess what? You already know how this feels. As children of our Heavenly Father, we have lost our memories of our premortal existence. Through the prophets and scriptures, we have learned about the great council in heaven regarding our earthly existence, agency, and the role of God and Jesus Christ in the plan of salvation. We have also learned how we decided to fight Lucifer and his followers by choosing the Lord's plan, which provided direction for His children to help them accomplish their missions on earth and to bring them safely back home.

We picked Heavenly Father's side because we knew and understood that Heavenly Father is going to win in the end. The fight is counting down to the close in these last days. Elder Boyd K. Packer said, "We can and in due time certainly will influence all of humanity.

It will be known who we are and why we are. It might seem hopeless; it is monumentally difficult; but it is not only possible but certain that we will win the battle against Satan."[1]

We are still in the midst of a war here on earth and we are coming up on the last battle. We need to be prepared with our greatest strength to help our Heavenly Father bring in the Second Coming of Jesus Christ.

While we are trying to prepare for struggles ahead, we need to remember that Lucifer has been in this fight much longer than we have. He's developed effective tools, skills, and lies over years of practice that are working well in these last days. The purpose of this book is to increase our awareness of these tactics and learn to combat them as a force for good (see Ephesians 6:11). Too often we allow Lucifer to use our strength against us because we don't recognize how strong we are through God and how weak Satan truly is.

The only way we can disarm Lucifer's efforts and understand his weakness is to be aware of the tools and lies he uses to tempt and corrupt us. Without being aware, we don't have to power to change. "Lucifer's attacks on the plan are intended to make the sons and daughters of God confused and unhappy and to ultimately halt their eternal progression. The overarching intent of the father of all lies is that all of us would become 'miserable like unto himself' (2 Nephi 2:27), and he works to warp the elements of the Father's plan he hates the most."[2]

Satan fights hard to make us all as miserable as he is. He is jealous of our mortality and our ability to progress and have families. Elder Jeffrey R. Holland said that

> Satan, or Lucifer, or the father of lies—call him what you will—is real, the very personification of evil. His motives are in every case malicious, and he convulses at the appearance of redeeming light, at the very thought of truth . . . he is eternally opposed to the love of God, the Atonement of Jesus Christ, and the work of peace and salvation. He will fight against these whenever and wherever he can. He knows he will be defeated and cast out in the end, but he is determined to take down with him as many others as he possibly can.[3]

We know from history that Satan has been successful in his destructive efforts. The scriptures offer examples that outline how Satan influenced people throughout time, for instance the Nephites shortly before Christ appeared to them in the Americas:

> The people began to forget those signs and wonders which they had heard, and began to be less and less astonished at a sign or a wonder from heaven, insomuch that they began to be hard in their hearts, and blind in their minds, and began to disbelieve all which they had heard and seen—imagining up some vain thing in their hearts, that it was wrought by men and by the power of the devil, to lead away and deceive the hearts of the people; and thus did Satan get possession of the hearts of the people again, insomuch that he did blind their eyes and lead them away to believe that the doctrine of Christ was a foolish and a vain thing. (3 Nephi 2:1–2)

Satan's power and destructive intentions are real, and we all need to be aware of Satan's tools to effectively combat him in the war for our souls.

Lucifer has unique advantages in his fight to sabotage us individually and the Lord's work collectively. Recognition and awareness of these advantages is essential for us to take appropriate defensive measures and action:

1. Lucifer is a master manipulator and liar.
2. His memory has not ever been taken away from him; he remembers everything from premortal life onward and he also knows each of us well.
3. We used to love him as our older brother.
4. He has been doing this for a long time, and practice makes a master.

Lucifer uses lies that are designed for these last days. These lies might not have worked as well earlier in history, but nonetheless they're working now. The reasons why these lies are so effective is that most of them have some measure of truth to them, like the half-truths that were previously mentioned. Because these lies have some truth to them, and because we are imperfect, it becomes easier for

Lucifer to pull us in and manipulate us into believing them. Some examples of these effective half-truths include:

- You need to be perfect and you're not.
- You're not good enough and never will be.
- The Atonement works for other people, but not for you because you've strayed too far.
- You should be able to fix yourself. What is wrong with you?
- You're thinking it, so it must be true; you are what you think.
- Other people are better than you (or you are better than other people).
- You are part of a chosen people so you deserve more.
- You should be able to forgive everyone automatically.
- You have made one too many mistakes. You're past the point of no return.
- If you get married in the temple, you're supposed to be happy.
- You deserve to be happy without any personal effort to become so.

Many people believe these kinds of lies. What makes them so effective and encompassing to so many individuals? The partial truth within them. Satan is using the truth found in Lord's gospel against His children, twisting it ever so slightly. We recognize the truthful part of the lie, which makes it much easier for Lucifer to convince us of the untruthful portion. This technique is working very well, so it's important to look at these half-truths individually in order to disarm them and take back our power.

Lucifer adapted his techniques as time and situations have changed. He has had a lot of time to hone his skills, techniques, and lies for the last days. For example, Lucifer understands the changes in our culture and the recent, expansive increase in technology. He utilizes his knowledge of mass media for destruction. He understands the exponential power that exists through this form of communication not only with individuals, but also with peers, groups, cultures, and countries. Elder Bednar recently taught about Satan's use of technology in today's world:

I raise an apostolic voice of warning about the potentially stifling, suffocating, suppressing, and constraining impact of some kinds of cyberspace interactions and experiences upon our souls. The concerns I raise are not new; they apply equally to other types of media, such as television, movies, and music. But in a cyber world, these challenges are more pervasive and intense. I plead with you to beware of the sense-dulling and spiritually destructive influence of cyberspace technologies that are used to produce high fidelity and that promote degrading and evil purposes.

If the adversary cannot entice us to misuse our physical bodies, then one of his most potent tactics is to beguile you and me as embodied spirits to disconnect gradually and physically from things as they really are. In essence, he encourages us to think and act as if we were in our premortal, unembodied state. And, if we let him, he can cunningly employ some aspects of modern technology to accomplish his purposes. Please be careful of becoming so immersed and engrossed in pixels, texting, earbuds, twittering, online social networking, and potentially addictive uses of media and the Internet that you fail to recognize the importance of your physical body and miss the richness of person-to-person communication. Beware of digital displays and data in many forms of computer-mediated interaction that can displace the full range of physical capacity and experience.[4]

Lucifer also understands how easily we can be influenced and affected by our cultural surroundings and the people in it. As technology steadily grows and people are more able to abuse and misuse it, there's a risk of Lucifer becoming more successful in his efforts and goals of individual and collective corruption.

The adversary uses mass media and technology to influence us collectively, but he also works to sabotage our potential individual power. How does he accomplish this? Lucifer wants us to believe that our power to choose is less than it really is. He is jealous and afraid of how we can influence ourselves and others through Christ and His light. Lucifer understands our power through Christ much more than we do. That is one of the reasons why he is working so hard to sabotage our self-esteem and make us believe we are less than we truly are.

Because of our human natures it's easy for us to believe that our influence isn't good enough or won't make a difference in the world, especially when we see how small we are in comparison to how many people are in the world now and how many people have been on it. But we may not realize the power we already have. Quantum mechanics says that everything we do has an effect on the world and call this process "the butterfly effect." This effect explains that the fluttering of a butterfly's wings can affect climate changes on the other side of the planet.[5] No matter how insignificant our choice to follow the Savior may seem, it could have long-lasting and powerful consequences.

If something as small as a butterfly can have such a far-reaching effect, imagine what we as individuals have the power to accomplish with the Lord behind us. The possibilities are endless. The Lord explained that we could literally move mountains from one spot to another with enough faith (see Matthew 17:20). Lucifer understands this individual power through Christ and works daily to disrupt our efforts by attacking our self-worth and self-esteem with some of his best tools.

How do we disarm Lucifer? We need to recognize and accept our power as well as his weakness. He is at his weakest when we have Jesus Christ as our greatest strength. He is the source of all light. Our power becomes great individually and collectively as we choose to follow Christ and His teachings.

The Apostle Paul spoke eloquently about our power through Jesus Christ.

> Who shall separate us from the love of Christ? Shall tribulation, or distress, or persecution, or famine, or nakedness, or peril, or sword? As it is written, for thy sake we are killed all the day long; we are accounted as sheep for the slaughter. Nay, in all these things we are more than conquerors through Him that loved us. For I am persuaded, that neither death, nor life, nor angels, not principalities, nor powers, nor things present, nor things to come, nor height, nor depth, nor any other creature, shall be able to separate us from the love of God, which is in Christ Jesus our Lord. (Romans 8:35–39)

I have found through my work as a counselor that immense power is available to me when I look toward Christ for guidance and seek Him for healing and strength, for myself and the clients I serve. This power is available to us daily. All we have to do is ask. As followers of Christ, we have the ultimate advantage over Lucifer because we know the outcome of the battle. Heavenly Father will win. Our challenge is to choose the correct side to fight for and align our attitudes and actions to our choice.

By taking a closer look at the adversary's effective tools, we can take the necessary action to disarm him. Awareness along with positive action will begin to accomplish the personal goals we make and free us from Lucifer's influence.

During my youth, I remember someone once saying to me that I need to be careful of what I want, because I might just get it. I sometimes explain the same concept to the youth I work with who are struggling to find their way in the world. It's difficult for these kids to see the effects of their actions on the future because, from what I have seen, young people tend to live in the moment.

I've asked them to picture themselves driving and looking to their right at a field of cows. If they didn't make the necessary adjustment of again looking to the road, pretty soon they were in the field with the cows. This is similar to how our choices lead us either toward Christ or toward Lucifer. We get to our destination based on our decisions. So it's important to know where we're going and to take one step after another until we are successful. We have been promised success through devotion and dedication to our Heavenly Father (see D&C 59:23). What a great promise!

We know we've chosen the correct team, so with that decision to follow the Lord, what makes Lucifer's influence on us so difficult to resist and dodge sometimes? He has found some great tools that are working for him and on us.

As in anyone's toolbox, we find the tools that work well and they become our favorites. We use them more often than others because of their effectiveness and durability. Lucifer's toolbox is the same. In Lucifer's toolbox, guilt is his hammer.

Many fall into Lucifer's web of guilt. It's easy to do because guilt is one of the half-truths. We are supposed to feel bad when we have done something wrong. So guilt becomes an effective half-truth for Lucifer to manipulate us. As said in the first chapter, some biological reasons exist as to why we feel guilt until we take the necessary steps toward healing, awareness, and understanding. Lucifer knows all of this and uses the knowledge to his benefit.

When we understand the difference between guilt and remorse, then it becomes our decision to follow the Savior. It becomes possible for us to forgive ourselves of the mistakes we make and have made in the past. We can move forward step by step, in a healthy manner, toward the goal of eternal life and returning to our Heavenly Father's presence.

5

Satan's Favorite Half-Truths

Half-Truth #1: Guilt and Comparison

We often fall into Lucifer's guilt trap because we compare ourselves to others. With this comparison we begin to believe we're not good enough and never will be good enough. Lucifer loves this half-truth. He wants us to feel that we're not as good as other people we see in our lives. The ironic is we only see the face of those people. We don't know what they're thinking, what they have done wrong. Because we can only see a small glimpse of them, we don't know them or their thoughts, feelings, or struggles.

Like traveling through a desert without food, water, and shelter, we begin to see things that might not be true. We believe there may be an oasis, but it is only an illusion. When we compare ourselves to others, we can only base it on our perception, which is not accurate because we don't have all the facts.

As we have a tendency to compare ourselves with others, it's important to remember where we're heading toward. We are all currently trudging through the mud field with the goal of getting across it and reaching a state of happiness and security. We're strong enough to do it only if we keep looking toward Christ, who is directing us on how to get through. Without His direction, we become lost and can't see clearly, especially during our trials. Sometimes the fog and winds seem overwhelming. Christ only asks for one simple thing: take one step and then another toward the garden (see 2 Nephi 31:20). We need to keep our focus on Him and never stop because when we stop we sink.

Through this trek, we become dirty. Never once are we clean. We look at the thousands of others struggling through the mud. Not one of them is clean either. Not one of them is better than any other. If we stop and lose direction, each one of us has the possibility of sinking. We have the opportunity each week to go to church and be edified. If we were all perfect we wouldn't need the sacrament or the Savior. But we're constantly making mistakes, so there is a constant dependency.

Problems can occur when we stop to look at others on their own quest through the mud, for the purpose of evaluating their progress. This is different than looking to others for the purpose of serving or helping them. When serving others, we're focused on Christ. It doesn't slow us down. What becomes disadvantageous and dangerous is when we slow down to look at others for comparison. Sometimes we think they are better than us or that we are better than they are.

This is a lie. This is one of Lucifer's favorite lies. Let's take a better look at this. Remember, when we're in the mud field, no one is less dirty than any other. It's impossible to be less dirty; we're all in the mud. No one has access to cleansing water. Sometimes people might look better than us because they're too far away and we can't see their situation. Sometimes they are further ahead in the mud, closer to the garden. Being closer doesn't make them cleaner or better than us. They are simply closer to their goal. They were once right where we are.

For example, I'm getting older and that puts me closer to the garden than my grandson, who is only ten. My grandson and I are both equally dirty from the mud, but I'm probably closer to accomplishing my mission on earth because of my age. Many children die young and have already fulfilled their missions in mortality at that young age, but while they were on earth they were muddy like the rest of us. Some of us simply have longer missions to accomplish here.

The same is true if we are looking at the people behind us, thinking we might be better than they are. Again, this is not so. We were once right where they are. If we think we're better than others, Lucifer has as much of a hold on us as when we feel incapable. Both of these conditions result in decreased self-esteem and self-worth, which Lucifer loves. Sometimes the sins that can be seen or smelled, such as drugs and alcohol, are easier for us to judge as a society, but realistically, if sin did stink, then we would all reek.

We lose our focus when we look at others for the wrong reasons. We might even start seeing what we want to see, but just because we think we see it doesn't make it true. We are all in the mud. None of us are able to wash ourselves clean.

Our perceptions can cause misunderstandings and difficulties if we are not careful and remain unaware of what is truly happening around us. Here is an example of how easily we can be misled by personal perception: I ask my clients to imagine themselves on the side of the road, stuck in the rain with a flat tire. Along comes one of their best friends, who looks them right in the eye and drives past. Then I ask them to imagine how they'd feel about this friend at that point in time. I generally get all kinds of negative responses and comments on what a real friend would do in the same situation. I then ask them to look inside of the vehicle as it is speeding past them standing in the rain. They look inside and see a bleeding child. *Now* how would they look at the situation? I normally get quite different responses than before.

Each of us is unique and we all have different circumstances, relationships, and backgrounds. Perception is not reality. We generally don't have all of the facts, regardless the situation. Risk levels increase with comparisons made by inaccurate perceptions.

Comparisons cause us to focus on being more like someone else, diverting our attention away from being more like Christ. This stops our progression, which is Satan's purpose.

As we keep moving and focusing on Christ we gradually become better people. This is an ongoing process, and daily habits outweigh any Herculean one-time effort. Remember, we don't have to be perfect to gain salvation.

Elder Bruce R. McConkie explained this truth in a beautiful and understandable manner when he stated that

> everyone in the Church who is on the straight and narrow path, who is striving and struggling and desiring to do what is right, though is far from perfect in this life; if he passes out of this life while he's on the straight and narrow, he's going to go on to eternal reward in his Father's kingdom.
>
> We don't need to get a complex or get a feeling that you have to be perfect to be saved. You don't. There's only been one perfect person, and that's the Lord Jesus, but in order to be saved in the kingdom of God and in order to pass the test of mortality, what you have to do is get on the straight and narrow path—thus charting a course leading to eternal life—and then, being on that path, pass out of this life in full fellowship. I'm not saying that you don't have to keep the commandments. I'm saying you don't have to be perfect to be saved. If you did, no one would be saved. The way it operates is this you get on the path that's named the "straight and narrow." You do it by entering the gate of repentance and baptism. The straight and narrow path leads from the gate of repentance and baptism, a great distance, to a reward that's called eternal life. If you're on that path and pressing forward, and you die, you'll never get off the path. There is no such thing as falling off the straight and narrow path in the life to come, and the reason is that this life is the time that is given to men to prepare for eternity . . . If you're on that path when death comes—because this is the time and the day appointed, this the probationary estate—you'll never fall off from it, and, for all practical purposes, your calling and election is made sure.[1]

Elder Neil L. Andersen also spoke with clarity on this topic in a conference address.

> Perfection does not come in this life, but we exercise faith in the Lord Jesus Christ and keep our covenants. President Monson has promised, "Your testimony, when constantly nourished, will keep you safe." We push our spiritual roots deep, feasting daily on the words of Christ in the scriptures. We trust in the words of living prophets, placed before

us to show us the way. We pray and pray and listen to the quiet voice of the Holy Ghost that leads us along and speaks peace to our soul.[2]

Elder McConkie and Elder Anderson elucidate that we won't and can't obtain perfection in this life. The purpose of mortal life is to stay focused in the right direction, knowing that we are always going to be making mistakes. When we do make mistakes, it might be better for our self-esteem if we gently brush ourselves off and begin walking toward our goal again.

Have you ever watched a toddler become a master at walking? At first, the child cannot walk at all and the goal is to learn. While the child is learning to walk, he falls at first, maybe getting bruised up a bit or even a few stitches. As the child practices, he gets better and faster. The point is the child doesn't beat himself up for not accomplishing this goal at a faster rate, nor does he compare himself to others as he is working on his goal.

A beautiful story from an unknown author illustrates what we so often do. We're really good at feeling the need to be more and to do more, especially when we feel inadequate inside. But one way or another, we learn that Christ is the only means of being the person we want to be.

One sister, Joan, was struggling with cancer and believed she was close to death. But she felt she hadn't done enough, felt she was unworthy, unready to die. As she sent up silent prayers of remorse for her inadequacy and shortcomings, what came back to her was a sweet, calm assurance that she was enough. The Lord impressed upon her that the daily, weekly, monthly assignments—like family home evening, scripture study and prayer, visiting teaching, and temple attendance—that she was using to measure her work and worthiness were actually gifts, gifts from Him for her to take advantage of, to help her, to bless her, not whips to beat herself with. Charity brings relief.

The Lord loves us so much that He has given us wonderful aids to help us better ourselves and bring us closer to Him. We don't read the scriptures and hold family night and say prayers to check off a list or receive a grade. We do them because they change us, bless us, teach us. We are not loved of the Lord by incremental scorekeeping—65 percent affection in exchange for 65 percent visiting teaching, 30 percent love granted for 30 percent scripture study, 80 percent blessings in answer to 80 percent daily prayer or temple attendance—we are just loved by the Lord, period. His ability to love us in our imperfection is part of what makes Him the Lord. The more we come to know Him, the more we know He loves us.[3]

I often use an analogy to demonstrate this principle to my clients. I have them picture both of us on the straight and narrow path, with Christ standing at the end, waiting for us to reach Him. Christ explains that the only thing we have to do is to stay on the path until we reach Him. We become excited, and despite the path being narrow, we believe we can accomplish this task. We begin walking toward Him, excitedly calling out to each other along the way. All of a sudden, an intense fog hits, so dense that we're unable to move because we can't see our next step. Also, the winds start blowing so hard that we feel we're about to lose our footing. We scream to the top of our lungs for help and Christ hears us calling for Him. He acknowledges us and says He will help us. He is going to give us each a tool, a sturdy walking stick. We breathe a sigh of relief and thank Him because we realize this is exactly what we need to be able to remain on the path. It will steady us when the winds become too strong and allow us to feel the path ahead when we cannot see clearly through the fog.

I then question my clients about what this walking stick might represent in their lives. They often come up with wonderful answers like scriptures, prayer, temple attendance, church attendance, visiting teaching, home teaching, family home evenings, and the Atonement.

But instead of using the walking stick the way that the Lord intended us to use it, we begin to beat ourselves over the back with it. Satan comes along to make sure we feel that heavy guilt and we feel like we deserve the pain. At that point, how helpful will the stick be for us? Christ would have us accept and apply these gifts in the manner that He intended them to be used. He gave us these gifts to use when we need comfort and strength to continue on our journey back into his arms, not as a tool to beat ourselves with. We don't need to be perfect to employ these gifts. They are there to buoy us when we need them.

President Joseph F. Smith, in *Gospel Doctrine*, said, "We do not look for absolute perfection in man. Mortal man is not capable of being absolutely perfect."[4] And Elder Joseph Fielding Smith also spoke on the subject: "Salvation does not come all at once; we are commanded to be perfect even as our Father in Heaven is perfect. It will take us ages to accomplish this end, for there will be greater progress beyond the grave."[5]

Jesus did not command us to be perfect to taunt us, but instead to teach us the truth of eternal progression. It was a message given to instill hope in what we can become through His help. However, Satan has turned it into a half-truth, teaching that if we're not absolutely perfect, we can't be saved. This is not true, but it does cause many people I have had the opportunity to work with to have difficulty even attending church services. I remember several women who would not attend church on Mother's Day. They explained that they felt intense guilt during the services because many of the Church members spoke of their wonderful mothers. They would acknowledge and remember the numerous mistakes they made while parenting their own children.

I believe these women were being too hard on themselves. I explained that we all make mistakes parenting children, and that complete healing and resolution of this pain will happen only through the Atonement of our Savior. This safe haven is where all healing occurs.

Many women I've worked with have also reported that they have, in the past, had trouble sitting through missionary farewells because of the way they were previously structured. At one time, these farewells were meetings where family members and parents often glorified the missionary by focusing on his life accomplishments. We know everything good that we're able to accomplish comes through the Spirit and power of Christ. In these farewells, however, the focus was more about the missionary. During these meetings, mothers would say with pride that all of their children have served honorable missions. Such statements were almost boastful, and mothers whose children didn't serve missions often felt guilt.

It's normal for us to praise children for positive behavior, but Church leaders have taught us to keep such conversations and extols at home in private, not during a sacrament meeting. I believe follow- ing this counsel decreases the possibility of guilty feelings for parents striving to do what is right but who might be struggling with a child's behaviors. Following this advice creates an environment conducive toward placing the glory where it belongs: with the Savior.

Gerald N. Lund explained the following: "Remember that one of Satan's strategies, especially with good people, is to whisper in their ears: 'If you are not perfect, you are failing.' This is one of his most effective deceptions, for it contains some elements of truth. But it *is* deception nonetheless. . . . He [God] wants us to strive for per- fection, but the fact that we have not yet achieved it does not mean we are failing."[6]

There are countless different situations where we as members look toward others when we should be looking toward Christ. For example, I remember a particular Sunday School class that I was attending where a teaching moment led to hurt feelings. Our won- derful teacher was reading the Proclamation to the Family,[7] spe- cifically the part where it discusses the importance of family time, family home evenings, and consistency in these events. He stopped at that point and singled out a young family. He mentioned to them, and to the congregation, that he knew this family was consistent in these goals because of the behavior of their children. He specifically asked them to state what time they held daily scripture study, family prayers, and family home evenings. He was essentially making the point that he knew this family accomplished these goals because of the children's outward behavior.

Though this was done in innocence, we need to be sensitive and careful about placing such labels on individuals and families. Say one of the children decided to stray, the parents would most likely believe it was because they didn't do something right. Or if other children are not as well behaved as these children, then other par- ents might feel like they are being judged for their parenting style or circumstances.

Many of the parents attending this class could possibly feel horri- ble about their own parenting history and how their children "turned out." This situation creates a perfect playing field where the adversary can run with these feelings, producing decreased self-esteem. When we hold on to these negative feelings, it decreases positive energy required to accomplish what we are sent to earth to do.

Heavenly Father is the greatest parent of all and He lost one third of His children because He allowed agency. It's not effective to judge parenting skills on the children's behaviors. I have worked with numerous individuals who have been consistent with family prayers and family home evenings yet whose children have strayed from the Church.

Lucifer is looking for every little situation where he can worm his way into our thoughts to distort the truth with guilt. We need to protect ourselves from Lucifer and his tactics. We have to treasure and understand who we are and our divine nature as children of God with continual awareness of who we are meant to be and where we are going. Lucifer is skilled at wanting us to believe we are less than our heritage as children of God. In essence, as he tries to destroy our self-esteem, the adversary is trying to steal our spiritual identities.

Robert C. Oaks said, in his talk about our eternal identities, that

today we receive many warnings about identity theft. . . . I am not talking about addresses, credit cards, or any other identifying numbers. I am talking about something much more basic and more important than who the world thinks you are. I am talking about who you think you are.

We know we are sons and daughters of God, with the potential to become like Him. . . . We also know that Satan is totally dedicated to thwarting and derailing this marvelous plan-of-happiness knowledge and process. We know that one of his primary tools is to entice us to forget who we really are—to fail to realize or to forget our divine potential. This is the cruelest form of identity theft.

How does Satan do it? He is quite straightforward and predictable. First, he attempts to prompt doubts in our minds about our divine potential. He even cultivates doctrine in the world implying we are much less than we really are. He undermines our faith—and thus our confidence—in our ability to achieve our potential.[8]

The ammunition that will stop the adversary right in his tracks is recognizing positive feelings of self-worth and remembering who we truly are. Robert Oaks continues, "One of the great blessings of understanding our true eternal identity as a child of God is that our personal sense of self-worth can only be high. He loves each one of His children. We are each His son or daughter, with the potential to become like Him."[9]

Positive self-worth and self-esteem, plus an understanding of our divine heritage and natures, create actual power that allow us to accomplish more, endure to the end, and work effectively with increased energy toward completing our mortal missions. We don't know what they might entail. They could contain undesirable, miserable conditions and tasks. We need both our energy and identities to accomplish our missions on earth. We can't let the adversary accomplish his identity theft. Our missions take real strength and trust to accomplish, not knowing exactly what they might require.

I've been through two personal experiences that have helped me to develop empathy and understanding about how difficult our earthly missions might be. The first involves my four sons. My two eldest both served missions. Their patriarchal blessings spoke in depth about their missions. My third son's blessing did not mention anything about a mission. I remember my second son, Brandon, attended the blessing with my husband and me. Brandon mentioned, as we were leaving the patriarch's home, the fact that my son's blessing didn't mention anything about his mission. We all acknowledged this and spoke about other parts we remembered about the blessing as we drove home.

My son who received the blessing that day was always a spiritual giant in our home. He attended his Church meetings without any promptings. He was an accomplished pianist, playing hymns on the piano almost daily, and was also successful in his schooling. Following his graduation, he made the decision to not serve a mission and "find himself." To say the least, I was shocked and devastated. I was broken-hearted. I expected and desired for him to learn from a mission and achieve the blessings that it might offer him.

During the time he was attending college, he began living with several roommates. At the end of the semester, as his roommates moved out, he and one woman were left alone in the apartment. As they became closer, they began reading the Book of Mormon together.

My son's roommate grew up in another religion, but as she read the Book of Mormon, she gained a testimony of it. She requested the missionary lessons. Long story short, my son ended up baptizing and later marrying this beautiful young woman in a civil ceremony. Within a year, her mother was also converted and baptized. Two years later, my son and his wife were sealed in the temple.

Years later, I was alone with him and questioned him about what caused him to fall away from the Church for that period of time, going through the trials and pain that resulted from that choice. He said with sincerity, "Mom, I always knew I would."

I said, "Really?" To which he replied, "Yes, ever since I was little."

My second example happened with one of my sisters. I grew up with eight siblings. One of my sister's main goals in life was to be married with many children. But sadly, she only had one beautiful daughter who was severely sexually abused when she was three years old. I cannot explain with words how distraught and devastated my sister was. My sister began to struggle with her testimony because she could not believe that a loving Heavenly Father would send this innocent child to Earth and allow this to happen to her.

She was angry with the Lord for years as she was healing from her pain. A strength and determination came about in my sister because of that horrific situation. My sister finished her schooling and became a therapist, specializing in counseling victims of sexual abuse. She has probably helped hundreds if not thousands of individuals, including her own daughter, instilling hope and a sense of peace through her years of counseling and public speaking engagements.

I'm not saying these were my son's and sister's missions in life, but I am saying it's possible. I know one thing when I reflect about what I went through with my son's struggles: that I could not have learned what I needed to know without going through this experience with him. I also know the Lord gave me the strength to endure that trial. We don't know everything about what our missions entail.

Elder Bruce R. McConkie explained about foreordination:

> The Lord foreordained chosen spirit children in pre-existence and assigned them to come to earth at particular times and places so that they might aid in furthering His divine will. These pre-existence

appointments, made "according to the foreknowledge of God the Father" (1 Pet. 1:2), simply designated certain individuals to perform missions which the Lord in His wisdom knew they had the talent and capacities to do. . . . In all this there is not the slightest hint of compulsion; persons foreordained to fill special missions in mortality are as abundantly endowed with free agency as are any other persons. By their foreordination the Lord merely gives them the opportunity to serve Him and His purposes if they will choose to measure up to the standard He knows they are capable of attaining.[10]

Carlfred Broderick, professor of sociology at the University of Southern California and a Church member, wrote in the *Ensign* that

so many children are abused, offended, and abandoned. If little children are precious to God, what justification can there be for permitting some to be born into such circumstances? . . . As children of God, we have been given the great gift of choice. We may choose to help, or we may choose to hurt. Unfortunately, as the Lord explained to Moses, the iniquities of one generation are often visited upon the heads of following generations. (See Exodus 20:5.) Anyone can see the truth of that saying by looking at many families in the world today. Often, troubled families seem to pass on their pain and darkness—virtually intact—to their children and grandchildren. The victim of one generation becomes the victimizer of the next.[11]

Indeed, my experience in various Church callings and in my profession as a family therapist has convinced me that God actively intervenes in some destructive lineages, assigning a valiant spirit to break the chain of destructiveness in such families. Although these children may suffer innocently as victims of violence, neglect, and exploitation, through the grace of God some find the strength to 'metabolize' the poison within themselves, refusing to pass it on to future generations. Before them were generations of destructive pain; after them the line flows clear and pure. Their children and children's children will call them blessed.[12]

In suffering innocently that others might not suffer, such persons, in some degree, become as "saviors on Mount Zion" by helping to bring salvation to a lineage.[13]

The following scriptures show how devastating some missions can be. Nephi was counseled to kill Laban so that millions of people would have access to the truth (1 Nephi 4:12–13). The prophet Joseph Smith was placed in Liberty Jail for an agonizing period of time (D&C 122:7–8). Joseph of Egypt was sold into slavery for years and served time in their jail (Genesis 39:20). Christ's mother, Mary, was pregnant out of wedlock in a time when she could have been stoned to death for that (Matthew 1:18–25). If we were there at that moment in time without knowing the final chapter, how would we look at each of these situations? Might we have had a tendency to judge these situations and individuals inaccurately? I believe the lessons learned in the scripture stories definitely apply to our own situations today.

However, when we compare ourselves to others, it inhibits our ability to receive necessary personal revelation for our own situations. We begin to live other people's lives. Comparing ourselves to others can inhibit essential personal knowledge, growth, and sometimes even personal safety.

The damage of comparisons is clear from what I have seen with my clients. People endure, sustain, and live with others who mentally, emotionally, or sexually abuse them without understanding how to escape from the abuse, until they are able to heal through the power of Christ and His Atonement. These families often look "perfect" from the outside. They usually have been married in the temple, attend their Church meetings on a regular basis, and have beautiful children.

However, these individuals end up being controlled, manipulated, and abused frequently. It becomes difficult to break away from these horrible situations because of embarrassment and not fitting into the mold of what they believe being an active LDS member entails. They often become afraid of rejection from the Church and begin comparing themselves to other individuals and families.

Situations such as this occur more than we realize. If we are open to the Spirit and personal revelation, the Lord can help us recognize what is important for us to accomplish. The Lord never expects us to stay in an abusive situation when safety is a factor. We are not expected to accept abuse.

Elder Richard G. Scott illustrated the importance of acquiring personal spiritual guidance in our lives.

Throughout the ages, many have obtained guidance helpful to resolve challenges in their lives by following the example of respected individuals who resolved similar problems. Today, world conditions change so rapidly that such a course of action is often not available to us. Personally, I rejoice in that reality because it creates a condition where we, of necessity, are more dependent upon the Spirit to guide us through the vicissitudes of life. Therefore, we are led to seek personal inspiration in life's important decisions.[14]

The Apostle Paul also explained the importance of personal insight and revelation and the danger of comparing ourselves one with another:

> Him that is weak in the faith receive ye, but not to doubtful disputations. For one believeth that he may eat all things: another, who is weak, eateth herbs. Let not him that eateth despise him that eateth not; and let not him which eateth not judge him that eateth: for God hath received him. Who art thou that judgest another man's servant? To his own master he standeth or falleth. Yea, he shall be holden up: for God is able to make him stand. One man esteemeth one day above another: another esteemeth every day alike. Let every man be fully persuaded in his own mind. (Romans 14:1–5)

Paul also stated, "For we dare not make ourselves of the number, or compare ourselves with some that commend themselves: but they measuring themselves by themselves, and comparing themselves among themselves, are not wise. But we will not boast of things without our measure, but according to the measure of the rule which God hath distributed to us, a measure to reach even unto you" (2 Corinthians 10:12–13).

The only way to know truth is through the Holy Ghost; it's never written by man alone. Even Peter, who knew Christ and met with Him and felt His presence daily, wasn't able to resist the urge to deny Christ when he was approached not once but three times. We are human and sometimes feel the same kind of doubt or fear that Peter might have been feeling, but we are counseled to listen and pay heed to our leaders and their guidance at all times because what they present to us is modern-day scripture and is always guided by the Lord.

On top of revelation from our leaders and modern-day apostles and prophets, personal revelation is available to all of us. We will remain safe if we look toward the Lord for guidance and do not judge ourselves, others, or our situations by other lives or our perceptions of their lives.

Half-Truth #2: Guilt and Our Thoughts

Lucifer uses the half-truth that we are who we think and not who the Lord thinks we are. This is not accurate. Because of our limited understanding and reasoning ability while we grow up, as mentioned before, we often have unresolved and unidentified emotional pain. Thoughts continually flow up from this pain without our recognition of the fueling emotions or situations. Some of them are extremely negative because of the nature of the pain behind them.

This pain built up as we grew because we couldn't effectively reason through our various situations. So these thoughts sometimes occur without a clear understanding of what might be their true source, and they can affect our actions until we understand how to manage or heal the pain that is causing dysfunctional thoughts and emotions.

A client of mine once explained that she was afraid of her father when she was young because he was reportedly gruff and often angry. When she was ten, he asked her one day to come to the kitchen sink so he could teach her how to make grape juice. The grape juice was frozen concentrate and he said that she needed to scoop out all of the frozen pulp from the can and put it into a pitcher. Nervously, she did what he asked and then he explained that she needed to put three ½ cans of water into the grape juice. She promptly placed the can under the faucet, filling it up. And because she wanted clean water in her grape juice, she poured out the water with the existing grape juice pulp down the sink. Surprised, her father yelled, "What, are you stupid?"

She internalized the thought and feeling that she was stupid. She couldn't understand that this situation stemmed from her father's problem, not hers. She reported to me that the beginning of her marriage was somewhat tumultuous, with ineffective communication. One day her husband made some kind of reference to her stupidity with certain behaviors. She emotionally exploded on her husband and let him know she was not stupid.

Her emotions emerged, led by the thought of her being stupid, which began during this childhood situation where she couldn't understand that her father was at fault. He might have had an argument with a good friend or not gotten enough sleep or any number of reasons for being grumpy and verbally abusive that day. But she internalized it as her being defective, and it affected her life until she was able to heal fully from the pain with the help of Christ and His Atonement. She wasn't in control of the emerging thought until she healed from that particular situation.

But it's important to understand that we are in control of the thought after it emerges. At that point, it becomes our decision on how to act from that thought. We are taught to "look unto Christ in every thought, doubt not, fear not" (D&C 6:36). Turning a negative thought toward Christ comes after the thought emerges.

The truthful part of this half-truth lies in that we are commanded to be stewards and to watch over our thoughts (see Mosiah 4:30). The Apostle Paul taught the following: "Casting down imaginations, and every high thing that exalteth itself against the knowledge of God, and bringing into captivity every thought to the obedience of Christ" (2 Corinthians 10:5).

This point is where Heavenly Father wants us to take control and maintain it after the thought comes, before we decide to act on it. Our Heavenly Father understands our mortality and understands this is where we do have control. After we are aware of the thought, we can take control of it and process it with healthy and effective behaviors. If we do, we can effectively become the steward over the thought and bring it to the obedience of Christ as the Lord would have us do. "Look unto me in every thought; doubt not, fear not" (D&C 6:36). We can direct our thoughts in a healthy, functional manner when we maintain control over our thoughts and following actions.

Half-Truth #3: Guilt and the Atonement

The Lord is bound by universal laws; one of them is justice, and another one is opposition in all things. There are always two ends of the spectrum. The atoning sacrifice of the Savior is at one end and justice for our mortality, which includes our imperfect carnal natures, is at the other. We're at the mortal end and we are stuck there without our Him. Everything good comes from His end of the spectrum. All light, all goodness comes through Christ. Our ability to be or do anything good comes from Him. He balances the equation through His sacrifice.

Opposition exists everywhere here on earth. Elder Richard C. Edgley said, "We live in one of the greatest dispensations of all times—a time former prophets looked forward to, prophesied of, and, I believe, yearned for. However, with all the heavenly blessings bestowed upon us, Satan, ever so real, is ever so active, and conflicting messages are continually bombarding all of us."[15]

Lucifer and his followers are the opposition. They works continually to convince us that there is no hope for us because we have sinned too much or too many times to ever be forgiven. This is another one of the half-truths Lucifer uses.

We hang onto our negative past feelings in an unhealthy way. We assume we have sinned too much to ever be forgiven. We know ourselves too well. We believe the Atonement works for everyone except us. We believe we're too evil and rotten. We see ourselves as being different than others around us. We often believe we are in the "valley of no return." We often tell ourselves these boldface lies. Lucifer wants us to internalize and believe them. He understands that most of us do believe these lies and tries to fuel them through his attacks on our self-worth and self-esteem.

We have the ability and strength to overcome the adversary's attacks in this area. We live in a world where everything light and good comes from Christ. Christ's light and strength surrounds us and is accessible to us every day. Part of the reason that so many believe the Atonement works for others and not for them is because they know themselves and they don't know others as well. All of fall into the trap of believing that we must have done more rotten, unforgivable sins than the other people we see around us who appear to be functioning well. However, all people struggle with adversity and have their own issues for which the Atonement becomes necessary. Everyone battles the same adversary. It's important to understand that we're not an exception from the Atonement. Christ already did the work, and if we focus on guilt, as the adversary would have us do, instead of remorse, we're rejecting essentially His sacrifice.

Jesus Christ knew we could not be saved except through Him. He agreed to save us from our mortality. We can't understand the impact of the Atonement for us until we understand that we can't do anything of good worth except it be through Christ (see Moroni 7:12).

Oswald Chambers wrote, "The greatest blessing spiritually is the knowledge that we are destitute; until we get there Our Lord is powerless. He can do nothing for us if we think we are sufficient of ourselves; we have to enter His Kingdom through the door of destitution. As long as we are rich, possessed of anything in the way of pride or independence, God cannot do anything for us."[16]

In Bruce Hafen's book, *The Broken Heart*, he said, "We sometimes say that the Lord will not save us *in* our sins but *from* them. . . . A sense of falling short or falling down is not only natural but essential to the mortal experience. Still, after all we can do, the Atonement can fill that which is empty, straighten our bent parts, and make strong that which is weak (see 2 Nephi 25:23)."[17]

Hafen continues, "This understanding is impossible without the experiences that teach us, sometimes painfully, about our own agency and independence. Paradoxically, it is only in discovering our independence from God that we understand our utter dependence on Him."[18]

An unknown author validated how great it can feel to give everything to Christ:

One by one, you hand Him your cares, sins, disappointments, illnesses, and imperfections. One by one, He embraces them and they melt in a puddle at His feet. You look down in awe as this pool of regrets evaporates and transforms into a glorious golden light that radiates out from Him in all directions. In the swell of that light comes a love more intense. It wraps you up in warmth and joy so remarkable that moisture fills your eyes once more. Only these tears are those of gratitude instead of guilt.[19]

Letting go of our perceived control and giving it to Christ, where it actually belongs, shows we are consecrating ourselves to the Lord. But what is consecration exactly? Merriam-Webster's dictionary defines *consecrate* as "to make or declare sacred, dedicate to the service of the Deity or dedicate to some purpose, to make something an object of honor or veneration."

Elder Neal A. Maxwell explains the importance of consecrating ourselves to the Lord: "These remarks are addressed to the imperfect but still striving in the household of faith. As always, my immediate audience is myself."[20] Here is an apostle of the Lord. His only job is to serve the Lord every hour of every day. Yet he acknowledges and accepts his weakness. We can't change anything we are not willing to acknowledge.

In Ether, it states, "And if men come unto me I will show unto them their weakness. I give unto men weakness that they may be humble; and my grace is sufficient for all men that humble themselves before me; for if they humble themselves before me, and have faith in me, then I will make weak things become strong unto them" (Ether 12:27). In the end, in order to overcome our mortality, it's essential to look to Christ for relief.

Every single person needs help beyond their own ability sometime during their lives, and God in His wisdom designed the plan of salvation with a Savior to atone for our sins and provide this help. Alma described it this way: "The Son of God suffereth according to the flesh that he might take upon him the sins of his people, that he might blot out their transgressions according to the power of his deliverance" (Alma 7:13).

Half-Truth #4: Guilt and Forgiveness

Another area that Satan uses guilt is with our limited knowledge and understanding of what is required to forgive. Forgiveness is not an automatic process. This is especially true if the wrongdoing was severe in nature. We do have to forgive, but we never have to remain with any kind of abuse. For example, if my sister killed one of my children, I would at some point have to forgive her of that horrific crime. But I would never have to be around her, or have any of my children around her again unless I felt the desire to do so. The Lord doesn't ever expect us to accept abuse of any kind. When we have experienced abuse, we may try to forgive but it's sometimes difficult to do.

We can find examples through the scriptures that teach this concept. Consider the example of Alma the Younger when he was causing destruction for the righteous by seeking to destroy the Church of God (Alma 36:14). Heavenly Father would expect us to stop this kind of abuse. It's up to us to protect ourselves from it, and that has nothing to do with forgiveness. We have to forgive, but we do not have to welcome abuse back into our lives.

Because we often believe that we should automatically be able to forgive, we fall into what is referred to as "the premature forgiveness cycle." This cycle can lead to depression, pain, or guilt.

The cycle starts out with the fact that we have been taught the necessity of forgiving. We have all heard examples of this in Church doctrine such as we need to forgive seventy times seven times (see Matthew 18:22), and the Lord will not forgive us if we cannot forgive others (see Matthew 18:35).

I had previously mentioned that growing up as my father's daughter was a fearful experience. His stunted growth as a child led to his limited parenting abilities, falling back on physical, verbal, and emotional punishment.

I attempted to forgive him, but I couldn't seem to forgive the abuse I'd received from my father. So I started to feel guilt and shame. I felt horrible. I tried to feel better by reading my scriptures, and what was I told to do? Forgive. I then felt more guilt. I attended Church again, hoping to feel better and I still heard the same forgiveness messages.

This premature forgiveness cycle pulls many individuals into the depths of depression and causes feelings of inadequacy. The adversary delights in this downward spiral, because we feel sad that we cannot quickly and readily forgive our enemies, which in turn makes us feel like we aren't keeping all of God's commandments.

The way to overcome this unnecessary guilt is to understand about what is required to be able to forgive permanently. Forgiveness is a step-by-step process, so to forgive others and move forward, we need to go through the steps.

Claigh Jensen, LCSW, explained the steps of forgiveness, which are listed below:

- Making the person you have to forgive human. (Which partially means understanding that this person makes mistakes just like the rest of us.)
- An awareness of and willingness to go through feelings of possible anger, hurt, pain, frustration, or humiliation.
- Willingness to apply the Atonement in our lives (2 Nephi 9:7).

As I proceeded to go through this process of forgiveness regarding my father's actions, I remember feeling anger toward him for the pain I received at his hands. My father died when I was twelve, so I was unable to work through these feelings personally with him. Nonetheless, there was a period of time when I was pretty mad at my dad. Being as close as I was with my siblings, I would often vent these negative feelings to them. However, their advice didn't always help me in my desires to fully forgive my father. I'm sure, in an effort to look out for me, my siblings would try to "save" me by saying things such as, "Karen, you need to forgive him, or you're going to go to hell."

I remember thinking at that point, *Oh well, then I guess I'm going to hell, because I'm still mad!* I had to take the time to process through these human emotions to forgive my father completely. Now I know I could see my father and run to him to embrace him and let him know how much I appreciate him and love him. This was a process that went well into my adult years before I could effectively heal and begin to understand and accept the Atonement in my life. At the point that I was finally able to forgive him, I was also strong enough to not allow more abuse.

I had to come to see him as a human, as a child that was hurt by his own father. I needed to view him as a child of God sustaining abuse of a severe nature. Being able to see his imperfect nature made it easier for me to forgive him. This was like watching the friend drive by when you're stuck on the road with car trouble. Your understanding of the whole situation is limited—you can't see the bleeding child in the car.

The hardest person to forgive, more often than not, yourself. We have to remember that the Atonement works for us as well as other people. Elder Jeffrey R. Holland stated the following regarding forgiveness: "'He who has repented of his sins, the same is forgiven, and I, the Lord, remember them no more' (D&C 58:42) . . . We can be so hard on ourselves—often much more than on others!"[21]

I frequently explain to my clients that we are abusive to ourselves on a regular basis. Many of the thoughts that come up aren't at all true but we still believe them. For example, if I forgot my daughter-in-law's birthday, it would be easy for me to tell myself that was a stupid thing to do and I should have been smarter by keeping track of the dates. This negative self-talk is common with people I've had the opportunity to counsel. I believe we would never talk to even our worst enemies the way that we sometimes talk to ourselves. I encourage my clients to talk to themselves the way they would talk to a good friend.

Heavenly Father is so merciful to all of His children. We are equally important in His eyes. He is not a "respecter of persons" (D&C 1:35). He wants us to forgive ourselves. He will help us accomplish this if we turn to Him, reaching out for help when needed, using the power of the Atonement for healing.

Lucifer, on the other hand, works both sides of a sin. He wants us to sin, so he will tempt us in every way possible to seduce us into doing something we know is wrong. After we have sinned, what we often don't realize is one of the adversary's greatest strengths is following up on the sin. He whispers to us, "See, I told you that you're rotten. You've always known you are. You've done way too much to ever be forgiven. You will never be good enough." He uses these negative thoughts in an attempt to destroy us.

Heavenly Father would never say anything like that. They come from Lucifer. Heavenly Father always has open arms, ready to hold and comfort us. This is the difference between guilt and remorse. The adversary wants us to feel and think that we can't ever make it, but the Lord wants to encourage us and help us realize when we're wrong so we can regain focus and make better choices.

Being able to forgive has a healing power. There's a well-known idiom that says if we cannot forgive it's like drinking poison and expecting the other person to die. It hurts us emotionally, spiritually, and physically more than anyone else. When we do effectively go through the steps of forgiving someone, it then becomes easier for us to forgive the next person. When we live a Christ-centered life, forgiving others and ourselves becomes easier because we are allowing the Atonement to work in our lives.

President James E. Faust relates the following story as an example of how living a Christ-centered life allows the power of forgiveness to work more quickly in a horrific situation:

> In the beautiful hills of Pennsylvania, a devout group of Christian people live a simple life . . . They are known as the Amish people.
>
> A 32-year-old milk truck driver lived with his family in their Nickel Mines community. He was not Amish, but his pickup route took him to many Amish dairy farms, where he became known as the quiet milkman. Last October he suddenly lost all reason and control. In his tormented mind he blamed God for the death of his first child and some unsubstantiated memories. He stormed into the Amish school without any provocation, released the boys and adults, and tied up the 10 girls. He shot the girls, killing five and wounding five. Then he took his own life.
>
> This shocking violence caused great anguish among the Amish but no anger. There was hurt but no hate. Their forgiveness was immediate. . . .
>
> Dr. Sydney Simon [said that] . . . "forgiveness is freeing up and putting to better use the energy once consumed by holding grudges, harboring resentments, and nursing unhealed wounds. It is rediscovering the strengths we always had and relocating our limitless capacity to understand and accept other people and ourselves."[22]

Forgiveness is a lesson that we are taught. It is a learning process, one that's not always easy or immediate. But it is one of the most beautiful gifts we can give to one another and especially to ourselves. The more we forgive, the more easily we can forgive in the future.

Most of us need time to work through pain and loss. I believe it's important to not berate ourselves for not being able to forgive automatically. When we put ourselves down, Lucifer starts to attack, which has the possibility of bringing us down further. Forgiveness is a process and with many things in life, practice makes perfect. The more we practice forgiveness, the better we become at the process. Remember, as long as we are trying we are being successful.

I also remember some sound advice from a loving bishop to a sister who had been through a painful divorce. This bishop encouraged her, saying, "Save a place in your heart for forgiveness, and when it comes, welcome it in." I think the most important part of this phrase is "when it comes." Sometimes we want it to be automatic and to jump forward in the forgiveness and healing process; however, forgiveness, like any process, takes time and effort.

If we are going through the process of healing and forgiveness or even trying to accomplish that task, then we are on the right track. The half-truth that Satan wants to have us believe is that if we cannot automatically have forgiveness in our hearts at all times, we are failing. This is not so. Elder Holland explained,

> Whatever your struggle, my brothers and sisters—mental or emotional or physical or otherwise . . . trust in God. Hold on in His love. Know that one day the dawn will break brightly and all shadows of mortality will flee. Though we may feel we are "like a broken vessel," as the Psalmist says (Psalm 31:12), we must remember, that vessel is in the hands of the divine potter. Broken minds can be healed the way broken bones and broken hearts are healed. While God is at work making those repairs, the rest of us can help by being merciful, nonjudgmental, and kind.[23]

And Elder Rex E. Pinegar said, "Further evidence of His love is that He gives you commandments to live. One of those commandments is that we should forgive others. He has said, 'I, the Lord, will forgive whom I will forgive, but of you it is required to forgive all men' (D&C 64:10). And that includes yourself! You must not count yourself guilty of that which you have not done."[24]

Half-Truth #5: Guilt and Perfection

The adversary constantly uses the "I'm not perfect so I must be failing" half-truth. In order to protect ourselves from this half-truth, we need to look at the full truth and accept our state of mortality.

Perfection, as we understand it, is obtained in our next estate. Everything we do of good worth in life is through the light of Christ. Our mortality is doomed without Him. Therefore, we are unable to attain perfection except it be through Christ. The real truth here is that we are not perfect, but Christ does not want us to feel guilty for that. He does want us to progress through the process of repentance and remorse. Lucifer does not.

Christ's and Lucifer's plan were opposite before we came to earth. In premortal lift we know that Lucifer presented a plan, saying, "Behold, here am I, send me, I will be thy son, and I will redeem all mankind, that one soul shall not be lost, and surely I will do it; wherefore give me thine honor" (Moses 4:1).

Lucifer wanted to restrict our ability to choose, thus attempting to force growth and development in exchange for his personal glory. But Jesus Christ had another plan, saying, "Father, thy will be done, and the glory be thine forever" (Moses 4:2). Christ wanted all to have agency and the ability to grow and develop and become like our Heavenly Father, which would bring us joy and peace. The account continues with Lucifer being cast down: "And he became Satan, yea, even the devil, the father of all lies, to deceive and to blind men, and to lead them captive at his will, even as many as would not hearken unto my voice" (Moses 4:4). So from that point onward, we had opposition in all things. Next, while visiting Adam and Eve in the Garden of Eden, "He sought also to beguile Eve, for he knew not the mind of God, wherefore he sought to destroy the world" (Moses 4:6). Satan thought that by convincing Eve to partake of the fruit that he could destroy the destiny of all who would come to the world, but because he didn't know the mind of God, he became central in the fulfillment of the plan of salvation. His opposition created the ability for Eve to make a choice between living in the paradise known as the Garden of Eden or to hard work in mortality, which would also bring growth and joy. The account states, "By the sweat of thy face shalt thou eat bread, until thou shalt return unto the ground—for thou shalt surely die—for out of it wast thou taken: for dust thou wast, and unto dust shalt thou return" (Moses 4:25).

I don't believe it was coincidence that this choice was presented to Eve as the mother of all. Without knowing exactly what was ahead, her motherly instincts probably hinted that the joy of having children and learning and growing to be like our Heavenly Father would far outweigh the pain and sickness and hard work of the process. So she chose a new way of life for her and her posterity, which Adam subsequently shared and supported. Of course we know the consequence of their choice, which is our mortality and our joy. "Adam fell that man might be; and men are, that they might have joy" (2 Nephi 2:25). Along with the capacity for growth and joy came the imperfect human side of mortality, with sin, opposition, death, and pain.

We have evil, carnal natures because of our mortality. We tend to fight this reality. We believe we have some ability to fix or to overcome this condition. We don't. In fact, if we believe we can fix ourselves, then there is no need for the Savior. We are in essence telling the Savior that what He did was not enough. His sacrifice was not enough to include saving us.

Nothing is further from the truth. There is nothing we as mortals could possibly do that can change this condition.

If we are not aware of this, we cannot fully accept the Atonement in our lives. We can't change anything we are not aware of. The Lord has said that dirt is better than us because it moves when He tells it to (see Helaman 12:7–8). Sometimes we don't move, holding onto the idea that we can help ourselves or that we must be strong enough to be able to do so.

It's absolutely vital that we embrace, acknowledge, and be aware of this fact: if we cannot embrace and accept our mortality, then we are constantly trying to change who we are, attempting to overcome this mortality on our own. We mistakenly believe we can save ourselves. If this were the case, we would have no need for the Lord and Savior.

Our goal is to be perfect even as our Heavenly Father is perfect (see Matthew 5:48), but we forget the eternal nature of our existence. This half-truth ensnares us because this state of perfection is not possible on earth. There have been billions and billions of people, but there has been only one perfect being that has ever walked on earth. We know that was Christ, and He was God's Only Begotten Son.

When we accept our weaknesses and imperfections and turn to our Heavenly Father in humility, we are made strong (see Ether

12:27). When we are submissive to His will in all things, we are made strong. When we desire to accomplish life's tasks on our own, it doesn't work. Submission is the key to strength. When we recognize we are weak without Christ in our lives, then we gain strength through Him as our Savior and all things are made possible.

I remember when my sons were young and growing up, I used to hear about what was required to go through boot camp in the military. I couldn't believe how mean this process was after I heard the details. How they would have to be totally submissive to the officers in charge of them and how they would be told to get down to the ground, to taste the dust, and follow all orders. I hoped my children would never have to go into the military because of boot camp. It sounded horrible to me for my sons to be placed in such a submissive, painful situation.

Years later, I became very ill. I tried everything to get better: attending doctor appointments over and over, holistic and natural remedies, exercising regularly, and trying to eat healthy meals. Years went by and no one could determine what was wrong with me. I ended up having a huge tumor in my buttocks that needed to be surgically removed during the worst part of my illness. I fought my illness extremely hard. I didn't want to die. I wanted to be here for my children and grandchildren. But, one day, I resigned myself to the fact that I could die. I gave complete power and submission back where it belonged—with the Lord. It was a total release of all my control and I became a willing servant of God. I was willing to die if that was what He wanted. I did not fight what might be His will anymore. And something wonderful happened. I started to get better. I realized at that point it is all right that we don't have any power. It's all right to be beaten down to the dust because at the point we realize we cannot do anything without His help. And then we become strong. Our strength is through our Lord, it always has been, and it always will be.

C. S. Lewis once said,

> The more we get what we call "ourselves" out of the way and let Him take us over, the more truly ourselves we become. . . . The more I resist Him and try to live on my own, the more I become dominated

by my own heredity and upbringing and surroundings and natural desires. In fact what I so proudly call "Myself" becomes merely the meeting place for trains of events which I never started and which I cannot stop. . . . Give up yourself, and you will find your real self. Lose your life and you will save it. Submit to death, death of your ambitions and favorite wishes every day and death of your whole body in the end: submit with every fibre of your being, and you will find eternal life. Keep back nothing. Nothing that you have not given away will ever be really yours. . . . Look for yourself, and you will find in the long run only hatred, loneliness, despair, rage, ruin, and decay. But look for Christ and you will find Him, and with Him everything else thrown in.[25]

The more we let go of the desire to be the best or the desire to be perfect, the stronger we become through letting Christ have the reins. And as we practice our faith by letting go of our desire to do it alone and the desire to be perfect, we become better, and then our progression continues in our next estate and on until the perfect day (see D&C 50:24).

Elder Neil Anderson also spoke about giving ourselves to Christ.

Jesus's call "Come, follow me" is not only for those prepared to compete in a spiritual Olympics. In fact, discipleship is not a competition at all but an invitation to all. Our journey of discipleship is not a dash around the track, nor is it fully comparable to a lengthy marathon. In truth, it is a lifelong migration toward a more celestial world. His invitation is a call to daily duty. Jesus said: "If ye love me, keep my commandments." "If any man will come after me, let him deny himself, and take up his cross daily, and follow me." We may not be at our very best every day, but if we are trying, Jesus's bidding is full of encouragement and hope: "Come unto me, all ye that labour and are heavy laden, and I will give you rest."[26]

Half-Truth #6: Guilt and Mistakes

We as humans make daily mistakes, which makes it easy to feel guilt, thus falling into Lucifer's traps. He teaches us that mistakes are not normal. He pulls us into the depths of despair, believing that we have made one too many mistakes. Like his previous half-truths, this one is false.

Mistakes and trials are opportunities for gaining wisdom and experience. A common expression states that there is no growth in comfort and there is no comfort in growth. If we are to become like God, we have to know everything. God is omniscient. We are here to learn as much as possible before we return back home to our Heavenly Father. I used to get angry and frustrated with Heavenly Father because of all of the trials I was going through. I didn't think he loved me much, until one day I recognized that I was gaining valuable wisdom, strength, and knowledge from my trials and tribulations. The prophet Alma spoke to his son Shiblon about the relationship between our faith, or trust in God, and the tribulations we encounter in daily life. He said, "I would that ye should remember, that as much as ye shall put your trust in God even so much ye shall be delivered out of your trials, and your troubles, and your afflictions, and ye shall be lifted up at the last day" (Alma 38:5). I think it's significant that Alma uses the words *as much,* meaning "to the degree" instead of the more commonly used "inasmuch," meaning "if." Reading the verse that way means that the Savior's power of deliverance is only limited by our own ability to trust in God.

President Henry B. Eyring explained further about the power of deliverance spoken of by Alma: "Now you might well ask, 'Since Heavenly Father loves us, why does His plan of happiness include trials that could overwhelm us?' It is because His purpose is to offer us eternal life. He wants to give us a happiness that is only possible as we live as families forever in glory with Him. And trials are necessary for us to be shaped and made fit to receive that happiness that comes as we qualify for the greatest of all the gifts of God."[27]

Our trials give us the opportunity to see the Lord's mercies in our lives. Nephi started out the first chapter of the Book of Mormon saying he wanted to show us that the tender mercies of the Lord are over all those who have faith, to make them mighty to the power of deliverance (see Nephi 1:20). Moroni ended the last chapter of the Book of Mormon saying we should remember how merciful the Lord has been to the children of men throughout history and ponder it in our hearts and ask God if they are true. He promised that God would manifest that truth by the power of the Holy Ghost (see Moroni 10:3–5). Recognizing the Lord's mercies in our lives can be a miraculous step in healing from our mistakes.

I realize how much Heavenly Father really does love me and how much He wants me to return home to Him. The more reliant on the Lord that I become, the more He molds and stretches me, and I become a stronger person through Him. I've earned this wisdom and knowledge through the mistakes and trials that I've experienced. It is the only treasure, along with my family and friendships, that I can take with me into my next estate. Heavenly Father loves each of us equally and wants the same for all of His children.

Child prodigies are naturally gifted in many areas, but never has a child been gifted with wisdom. Wisdom is earned through trials and overcoming mistakes. However, we all make mistakes every day. Instead of beating ourselves up because of our shortcomings, we can learn and grow from them.

I remember hearing a story about a little ten-year-old. He was a child prodigy who was gifted in music, able to play the piano beautifully by ear. Around Christmastime he was scheduled to play to an auditorium of people. He was the only one in that auditorium making hundreds of minor mistakes while playing the piano, but he was also the only one providing beautiful music. This little man was brave and willing to take the risk of making mistakes for his own growth and to bestow beautiful music for the enjoyment of others.

If we're afraid of making mistakes, we can't progress. Mistakes are, in a way, a blessing because there is actual power and energy behind them. The power and energy to either learn from the mistakes or to rot in the results. It's important to embrace them, accept what we have done, partake in Christ's power of deliverance, and learn and grow from the experience. We can't let ourselves sink.

Elder Robert D. Hales said,

All of us make mistakes. The scriptures teach us, "All have sinned, and come short of the glory of God" (see Romans 3:23). For those who find themselves captive to past unrighteous choices, stuck in a dark corner, without all the blessings available by the righteous exercise of agency, we love you. Come back! Come out of the dark corner and into the light. Even if you have to walk across a newly varnished floor, it is worth it. Trust that "through the Atonement of Christ, all mankind [including you and me] may be saved, by obedience to the laws and ordinances of the Gospel" (Articles of Faith 1:3).[28]

I see so many of my clients beating themselves up for past mistakes. Part of this abuse we throw at ourselves comes because of our conditioning as has been explained earlier, but part of it comes from the fact that we have actually learned something from our mistake. Imagine that! We're smarter than we were before, so we say to ourselves, "Why didn't I do that different?"

A possible reason why we made the mistake because it was the only thing we knew how to do at the time. Since we have become smarter from going through the mistake, and learning from it, we now start to beat ourselves up because we didn't already know what we learned from the mistake before we made it. Can you see how Lucifer could use this human reasoning? I can; I see it all the time with my clients. The analogy that I often use with them is a horse race. I explain that right now, at this point in time, they're in the winner's circle with the horse that won. They know which horse won because they're standing next to it. The problem comes when we beat ourselves up for not knowing which horse was going to win back at the gate. However, we couldn't guess the winner back at the gate, because we didn't know. Most people beat themselves up for not knowing which horse was going to win. It's impossible. There is no way we could have known. It's the same way with our mistakes. We made the mistake because we didn't know how to do differently and then we beat ourselves up for having the knowledge after the fact.

In my opinion, mistakes have made me rich, but not with money. I'm getting old enough in my life that now I can look back and recognize that the only treasure I will be taking with me to heaven is the wisdom and knowledge that I have learned through my trials. My treasure is what I have learned, and I have earned it. I'm so grateful to my Heavenly Father for knowing the trials I have needed and do need to be able to grow toward my ultimate goal of the celestial kingdom. My mistakes have been a huge part of my growth. I never could have learned what I needed to learn without making them. We can never make too many mistakes to turn the Lord away from us, no matter where we are in our progression.

The adversary desires for us to feel guilt from these mistakes. Instead of staying stuck in our guilt and misery, let's take back our spiritual power to learn and grow from our mistakes.

Sheri Dew's book *No One Can Take Your Place* shares an amusing explanation of how much power we actually have over the adversary. In it, a young woman came up to her, following her talk, and said, "Sister Dew . . . every morning when you wake up I'll bet the adversary says to himself, 'Oh heck, she's awake again.'"[29] We have the strength to cause Lucifer to tremble in his metaphorical boots as we follow Christ. Lucifer has reason to fear and loses his power when we carry the strength of the Lord with us in all that we do.

We have all the necessary tools to return home to our Heavenly Father, as stated by President Monson:

> We have been provided divine attributes to guide our journey. We enter mortality not to float with the moving currents of life but with the power to think, to reason, and to achieve . . . I speak of prayer. I speak too of the whisperings from that still, small voice; and I do not overlook the holy scriptures, which contain the word of the Lord and the words of the prophets—provided to us to help us successfully cross the finish line. . . . "The race is not to the swift, nor the battle to the strong" (Ecclesiastes 9:11). Actually, the prize belongs to him or her who endures to the end.[30]

Elder Holland presented one of the many parables Christ taught during his lifetime on earth:

> A householder "went out early in the morning to hire labourers." After employing the first group at 6:00 in the morning, he returned at 9:00 a.m., at 12:00 noon, and at 3:00 in the afternoon, hiring more workers as the urgency of the harvest increased. The scripture says he came back a final time, "about the eleventh hour" (approximately 5:00 p.m.), and hired a concluding number. Then just an hour later, all the workers gathered to receive their day's wage. Surprisingly, all received the *same* wage in spite of the different hours of labor. Immediately, those hired first were angry, saying, "These last have wrought

but one hour, and thou hast made them equal unto us, which have borne the burden and heat of the day."

This is a story about God's goodness, His patience and forgiveness, and the Atonement of the Lord Jesus Christ. . . . It underscores the thought I heard many years ago that surely the thing God enjoys most about being God is the thrill of being merciful, especially to those who don't expect it and often feel they don't deserve it.[31]

It is never too late to come unto Christ. It doesn't matter how many or what kinds of mistakes you've made, Christ's arms are always wide open, waiting for us to run toward Him for relief. We need to partake of the Savior's power of deliverance, to shift our thoughts from the mistakes we made to recognition that our Heavenly Father knows what is best for us. This will lead us to our eternal reward if we have humility and faith. Remember that the final judgment is not a judgment of our total goods and evil acts or what we have done. Instead, it is a judgment of the final effect of our acts and thoughts or what we have become. The power of deliverance will help you become what our Heavenly Father has in mind for you, regardless of who you might have been in the past. There is no deep, dark crevice where the infinite light of Jesus Christ's Atonement doesn't shine.

Book Three: The Lord's Plan for Joy

6

Joy versus Happiness

The Runner

Cliff Young, a man in his sixties from Australia, became famous overnight for winning a world-renowned race, beating many younger runners and breaking the race's record time by over ten hours. He gave away the prize money, stating that he did not enter the race for the money. This race has been referred to as the human version of the famous fable "The Tortoise and the Hare."

This man was unknown before the race. He reportedly grew up on a two thousand-acre sheep farm with thousands of sheep to care for. His family was poor and survived during the depression, running their farm with little or no advanced technological equipment. Cliff was forced to run daily to perform his expected tasks and to care for the sheep. Sometimes he'd have to run for two or three days straight without sleep to gather the sheep before an oncoming storm.

He would do all his daily running in gumboots and overalls. Day after day, year after year, he awoke to perform the same daily tasks of feeding and gathering animals. I'd imagine that though this became tedious and tiresome he also felt some joy of accomplishment as he was able to protect and feed the sheep.

Then one day in his sixties, he decided to enter a seven-day race. As he began running, many people thought him to be a bad runner because of his form; he ran with a shuffle. The other younger runners quickly ran far ahead of him but he continued at his steady rate. The normal sleeping quota for the runners was approximately six hours, which would leave them a running time of eighteen hours. Cliff continued to run through the nights without sleep because of how his body was conditioned. His body had become strong because of his willingness to accomplish his daily tasks on his farm. By the fifth day he was way ahead of the other runners and never gave up the lead. He crossed the finish line. He was reported to say that he knew he could do it and that death would be the only thing to stop him from running. Cliff was essentially doing his daily tasks that were asked of him on the farm. I'm sure there were times when he became tired or felt that what he was doing was unimportant, but accomplishment of his assigned tasks built a level of strength in him that was unbelievable. He was able to earn a great reward from his efforts when everyone believed the odds were against him and that he wouldn't be able finish.[1]

How does this story apply to us, our lives and joy and happiness? What's the remedy for the pain that is often continual through our trials? How do we achieve the joy that God has promised us that man might have (see 2 Nephi 2:25)?

Sometimes we're deceived into believing the wrong things can bring us the greatest joy such as being admired by other people or being in a position of power. It's a false pride and happiness. We have not been healed from past hurts, so we focus on the effects of an addiction (essentially a cover-up of our true feelings) because we don't feel comfortable with feeling who we are. The reason I know this is very personal. I've been there.

I grew up in a large group of siblings and we performed as a family while traveling all over the country singing, dancing, and playing instruments. Because of the way I was conditioned and acculturated, it was easy for me to be in the limelight, to speak to people in public, and to be the life of every party. Also, because of my upbringing, I always desired higher positions in the Church like teaching adults or being a member of the presidencies.

Such positions placed me in the spotlight where I was comfortable. Other people were focused on me and where I was. I was given the attention because I was good at getting attention. The problem with this situation is the fact that the focus was on me. Should it have been on me? No. To have true joy, the focus should be on Jesus Christ.

What I was feeling was a false sense of pride and happiness, which Lucifer magnified. The adversary tries to boast our egos. But it's short-lived, fleeting, and without the depth, understanding, and growth to sustain us and carry us through trials.

As we heal with our focus on Christ, true joy is possible, even on a daily basis. Something that sustains me over and over again happened when I was a Sunbeam teacher. When I was placed in the position, I wasn't excited about it. Also, I cannot say that every Sunday was filled with joy while fulfilling my Sunbeam calling. Sometimes I felt tired, unimportant, or frustrated, like Cliff, the runner, might have felt with his daily tasks.

For instance, one Sunday we were learning about animals and the lovely creations of our Heavenly Father. We were crawling around on the floor, pretending to be animals, when one of my cute little Sunbeams imagined he was a dog and bit a hole right through the middle of my skirt. That was one of many unique experiences during my time as Sunbeam teacher.

Most Sundays, I would come home exhausted and have to take a nap before even being able to cook dinner. I did not look forward to Sundays. They were a lot of work, and I missed my dose of admiration I'd received from others if I gave a talk or taught an adult lesson. At least that ego boost provided me with a little bit of adrenaline that would carry me through the effort of making dinner when I returned home.

But something miraculous happened one Sunday. This was a Sunday that I'll never forget. Ironically, this little miracle happened the last Sunday I was teaching my little group of energetic youngsters. Our classroom time started out pretty normal: I was on the floor (as usual), teaching the children our little lesson before we started coloring our pictures. The children were all in a semicircle surrounding me, listening intently (which was the biggest part of the miracle). I held up one of the pictures and began to explain another portion of the lesson when my big-eyed, sometimes angelic Anna quietly raised her hand. She held it there in the air for a few moments and waited for me to call on her. I stopped speaking and placed the focus on her and said, "Yes, Anna?" She then sincerely and sweetly said, "I love you!" Well . . . I burst into tears. The feeling in that room was overwhelming, the sweetest feeling I had ever felt. I told her that I loved her too. It doesn't get any better than that, at least not for me. It's a moment that brings me great joy every time I think about it. It has effectively carried me through some painful moments, and I will remember it all the days of my life.

Looking back on that experience, I realized what an effective analogy it presents regarding our lives here on earth. Almost always our lives are going to be difficult, tedious, or boring because there is no growth in comfort and no comfort in growth. We're sent here to grow and learn. Just as Cliff probably didn't recognize the strength he was building through what appeared to be mundane tasks, we are also building our strength through doing what the Lord has asked of us on a daily basis. Like how Cliff was rewarded for his efforts, I believe a reward is in store for our efforts. We gain valuable wisdom, strength, and rewards from serving the Lord.

In life, we don't know what is going to be around the next bend, like how I didn't know what was going to happen in my weekly Sunbeam class. I got tired every time I had to teach the Sunbeams. Often, it took all of my energy without seeing much marked progress or getting any kind of recognition or acknowledgement for all of my hard work. Much of life is like the experience I had of teaching Sunbeams. It is hard. Most of us work hard and get tired daily without much recognition or acknowledgement.

But I learned from the experience of teaching that joy can be found in all life's situations. That one fleeting expression of love from Anna still carries me through the drudgeries of life much more than any of the admiring remarks I'd received during my adult lessons or positions.

I believe the difference was that I was totally focused on Christ in that moment. I was not at all focused on myself. That is why the joy was possible. There wasn't any recognition or focus on me. When we place our focus on Christ and His teachings and His commandments, true joy is available in life. As I look back at my life, I notice that as I followed Christ, that is when my true joy came. It always comes as I follow Christ's wisdom and commandments.

The same is also true with the commandment the Lord has given all of us to multiply and replenish the earth. Joy has come often in my life through following this commandment—along with heartaches, daily mundane tasks without any apparent reward or relief, and hard lessons learned. But there are regular doses of joy as I'm surrounded by my children and grandchildren. Joy is daily with them. I call grandchildren the "chocolate of life," and I love chocolate.

Joy versus Happiness

Lucifer would like us to believe that we deserve to be happy in our lives without working for it. He uses it in tandem with the scriptural teaching of being chosen. He tells us that we are more special than others because we're the chosen people. It's easy to fall into this trap because we *are* chosen. But for what exactly? The truthful part of the half-truth is that we are chosen to accomplish the Lord's will by following Him, to do missionary work, and to help bring in the Second Coming of the Lord (see D&C 121:34–46). Because one of our purposes in life is to help bring in the Second Coming, the concept of us as a chosen people definitely carries with it a personal responsibility to earn it through our thoughts and actions toward God (see D&C 29:4–8). It isn't a blessing given without effort on our part.

In the Doctrine and Covenants, the Lord explains, "There has been a day of calling, but the time has come for a day of choosing; *and let those be chosen that are worthy.* And it shall be manifest unto my servant, by the voice of the Spirit, those that are chosen; and they shall be sanctified; *And inasmuch as they follow the counsel which they receive, they shall have power* after many days to accomplish all things pertaining to Zion" (D&C 105:35–37; italics added). God teaches us that we need to be worthy vessels in order to be chosen by Him to accomplish His will. He also teaches that by following His promptings in our lives, we are endowed with power from on high to help us accomplish whatever He asks.

We are also taught in other passages in the Doctrine and Covenants the difference between being called and being chosen. The Lord said, "Behold, there are many called, but few are chosen. And why are they not chosen? *Because their hearts are set so much upon the things of this word, and aspire to the honors of men*, that they do not learn this one lesson—That the rights of the priesthood are inseparably connected with the powers of heaven, *and that the powers of heaven cannot be controlled nor handled only upon the principles of righteousness*" (D&C 121:34–36; italics added). Where our hearts are truly is where our treasure is. Only righteousness and an eye single to the purposes of God through Christ's sacrifice can control the powers of heaven and make us His chosen. The Lord also speaks of our calling as missionaries (see D&C 29:4).

Some may think being an heir to the Abrahamic covenant makes us chosen. But the Bible Dictionary clearly says, "Being an heir to the Abrahamic covenant does not make one a 'chosen person' per se, but does signify that such are chosen to responsibly carry the gospel to all the peoples of the earth. Abraham's seed have carried out the missionary activity in all the nations since Abraham's day. (Matthew 3:9; Abraham 2:9–11)."[2]

But the Lord is no respecter of persons (see Romans 2:11). That means that everyone is equally important in Heavenly Father's eyes, no matter whom they are or what they do.

We are chosen to work. Where much is given, much is expected (see D&C 82:3). We're a chosen people, which is a gift, but we are saved after all we can do. Life is hard and all living things faces adversity. Adversity creates strength.

In this modern day, we are conditioned to believe we deserve to be happy, whether we earned it or not. This is especially believable with those who have made covenants such as baptism or endowments. This is simply not true in our mortal existence. We are required to work hard to achieve our rewards, including joy and happiness. That's one reason Heavenly Father commanded that cherubim be placed to guard the tree of life in the Garden of Eden after Adam and Eve had partaken of the fruit of the tree of knowledge. Happiness, joy, and eternal life are not merely given to us. We achieve these aspirations after all we can do (see 2 Nephi 25:23). The Lord has said that "men are that they *might* have joy" (2 Nephi 2:25; italics added), not men are that they *will* have joy. There is a big difference between those words. *Might* is an action verb and requires action and work. How we choose to live determines how happy we are in this life and the life to come.

With that in mind, what we're taught in our childhood becomes an important source of wisdom and instruction in our lives. This conditioning affects everything we do during our adult years. For example, if you had always put up your Christmas tree on Christmas Eve while your spouse was used to putting up the tree the day after Thanksgiving and taking it down in January, these two differences have the possibility of conflict. If we experienced pain during our childhood, as previously mentioned, it can affect what we do as adults unless we're willing to heal and then search, ponder, and pray for additional wisdom and guidance.

A classic example of our childhood conditioning, which causes us to assume that certain things should happen in certain ways, is the story of Cinderella. Many little girls base their hope for the future on the ending that this story presents. Who wouldn't? Cinderella finds a rich and handsome prince who rescues her from her former life of squalor by marrying her and they live happily ever after. Children believe the specifics of this story; for example, after marriage all of their problems will disappear. Because of this credulousness, it is our responsibility as parents to educate our children on the truth and condition them with a healthy understanding of this famous folktale.

We have to look at the specifics of this story to extract the truth from it. There are several versions of it, but I remember the following: Cinderella is born to a rich noble father who is a duke. Her mother died from sickness when she was young. She was raised alone by her father until he married a woman with two daughters, making them her stepsisters and the woman Cinderella's stepmother. Tragically, Cinderella's father died from illness and Cinderella became a servant, caring for every perceived minuscule need of her stepmother and stepsisters.

Cinderella is forced to reside in a filthy attic and her needs are treated as frivolous and unimportant. This disadvantaged situation goes on for many years until Cinderella becomes a beautiful, mature young woman. At that point in time, her sisters are invited to a grand ball hosted by the prince, but Cinderella isn't invited. After her sisters leave for the grand event, Cinderella is crying in her kitchen when her fairy godmother comes into the picture and uses her magic to allow Cinderella to go to the ball. She does go, and Prince Charming and Cinderella fall in love. Cinderella's magic disappears at the stroke of midnight and she runs from the ball when she hears the clock start to chime. As she is running, she loses one of her glass slippers. Ultimately, Prince Charming finds the slipper and takes it from house to house trying it on all of the eligible young women in his kingdom until Cinderella is identified. The prince rescues her from her horrible situation, they get married, and they naturally live "happily ever after."

Children have false expectations about how to achieve their own happy ending because no one ever explains the rest of the story. They don't understand all of the things that could happen within or before marriage. So when problems surface later in their lives, they wonder why they aren't happy or how their happy endings slipped through their fingers.

Carol Lynn Pearson wrote a wonderful book called *The Lesson: A Fable for Our Times*. She identifies in it a few problems that could possibly happen during the course of a lifetime. The following are a few examples of such problems:

What if you were a teenager and you weren't doing well in school, or you weren't popular, or you had pimples all over your face, or your parents were getting a divorce and you thought it was your fault? What if you really wanted to go to college and it cost five thousand dollars but you only had two thousand? What if you had three children, and one of them was born with a birth defect that added to your sorrows because it subtracted from her possibilities and divided your attention and multiplied the problems of caring for your family? What if you knew that your boss at work was cheating forty-five people . . . and if you said anything there would be a ninety-percent chance you would lose the best job you'd ever had? What if your body had three heart attacks and one missing kidney and you got weaker and weaker until you could hardly breathe . . .[3]

What makes us believe we aren't supposed to struggle and fight for our survival? We live in a trauma-based world. Every living thing faces opposition, down to the leaves on the trees that need to struggle against the wind. We live in a society where we are conditioned to believe that we deserve to be happy. Lucifer is behind this.

Elder Robert D. Hales said, "The world teaches many falsehoods about agency. Many think we should 'eat, drink, and be merry; . . . and if it so be that we are guilty, God will beat us with a few stripes, and at last we shall be saved.' Others embrace secularism and deny God. They convince themselves that there is no 'opposition in all things' and, therefore, 'whatsoever a man [does is] no crime.' This 'destroy[s] the wisdom of God and his eternal purposes.'"[4] The eternal purposes mentioned here are to bring to pass the exaltation of man, and in these last days help to bring in the Second Coming (see Moses 1:39). Lucifer wants to destroy both of those goals. He wants us to believe we can play instead of work toward Heavenly Father's plan. He tries to make us believe that playing is more enticing and more beneficial both in the short term and also in the long run.

One of the reasons Lucifer has such power with the concept that we deserve to be happy is because it's true that we deserve to have joy and happiness, only after working for it. But we are going about it the wrong way. Because of Lucifer's work, we believe joy can come to us through worldly things, instant gratification, and easily-managed relationships. However, everything worthwhile is worth working for. Nothing on earth is a given or it wouldn't be an effective classroom.

We also live in a society that assumes if bad things happen to us, then we must be doing something wrong and we're being punished. The real truth is that bad things happen to good people all of the time. Because there is wickedness and hatred in the world around us, some of it will be directed toward us from time to time. However, adversity brings strength and wisdom. Opposition becomes a good thing if our goal is to learn to be like our Heavenly Father.

Bruce R. Hafen explained,

> When we first realize we have a testimony, the amount of spiritual truth we know could be symbolized by coloring in a tiny circle about the size of a pinhead. As our understanding progresses, the circle

grows. When our knowledge develops to a certain point of maturity, the circle may be the size of a coin—many times bigger than our first little pinhead of knowledge. . . . In the larger circle, the much longer circumference around the edge of the circle now puts the testimony in much greater contact with the unknown. Thus, there are many new points at which questions can arise. The more knowledge we gain, the more potential opposition we face. But it is through the "growing pains" of dealing with that opposition that our knowledge and understanding increase geometrically.[5]

So the more we know, the more we have access to knowledge, and if knowledge and growth are a byproduct of adversity, then it only makes sense that our adversity would be increasing as we gain wisdom. In fact, opposition grows as someone becomes more valuable to the Lord's purposes. The Prophet Joseph Smith and many others knew that well. When he was incarcerated in Liberty Jail, the Lord said, "Know thou, my son, that all these things shall give thee experience, and shall be for thy good. The Son of Man hath descended below them all. Art thou greater than he?" (D&C 122:7–8.) Since God is all knowing and we're on the quest to become Gods, we have a lot to learn. So we are in the right place.

If adversity is a constant in our lives, there must be some correlation to happiness and the joy we have been promised (2 Nephi 2:23). We are told to marry and reproduce and are conditioned that this marital union and having children will result in joy and happiness.

Bruce R. Hafen said,

Many young people assume if they can just get married, all their problems will be solved. . . . I think of a young couple standing on a soggy lawn at the Idaho Falls Temple one beautiful spring day to have their pictures taken following their temple marriage. It was a picturesque scene, until the groom inadvertently stepped on the ruffled hem of the bride's white gown, mashing it into the wet, muddy grass. She gently asked him to move his foot, but he was too happy to hear her. She needed to speak with more intensity, and both were embarrassed. Then they had little choice but to stand through the reception a short time later, hoping to conceal the smudge that suggested, symbolically, that even a temple marriage has its share of opposition—from the beginning.[6]

Because of how our society has raised us, we tend to believe we deserve to be happy and that comes with instant gratification. This could include material things that might make our lives easier, but instant gratification often actually damages our lives and especially our marriages. Our conditioning kicks in when we get married and become unhappy married because of misconceptions, which can ultimately lead to divorce.

I'll never forget one of my sons approaching me as he became close to a young woman whom he was considering marrying. He was afraid, explaining to me that he had seen many of his friends get married before him and none of them appeared happy. I told to him that marriage is a growing process that God intended us to have so that we could learn valuable lessons toward of goal of Godhood. My son already understood that marriage was an essential step for his progression but he wanted to be happy doing it. He is learning that happiness and joy come from hard work. The possibility of joy and happiness comes from the full spectrum opposites, including pain and suffering. Remember, the Lord is bound by universal laws, one of them being opposition in all things. We have to have the possibility of pain and sadness to have the chance to experience joy.

Bruce R. Hafen continues to explain,

> Those who . . . veer away from the demanding course of the life cycle at the first sign of pain or bitterness may never experience the humility, the soul-searching, the sensitive reaching out, and the reconciliation that come in finally understanding things from the perspective of another person, or in subordinating one's own needs to those of another. . . . On the other hand, those who remain committed enough that leaving is not an alternative are likely to make remarkable discoveries about their spouses and about themselves. Significantly, these discoveries may have profound effects upon their own personal maturation and development.[7]

Hafen continues, "Experiences such as these may surely lead toward living joyfully, but joy—like grace—comes 'after all we can do' (2 Nephi 25:23). Indeed, joy—like grace—may well come in the midst of contrary experience, for it is a real part of life. Joy is not an alternative to opposition; it is part of a compound that includes opposition."[8]

Many marriage partners, whom I've had the honor to counsel over the years, reportedly become tired of the routine of daily life raising a family. Too often the marriage can break up because one of the participants decides that he or she wants to be "happy." Marriages, especially eternal marriages, become targets for the adversary. He knows the power that a strong marriage and family will continue to have through many generations. If he can break up an eternal marriage, destroy a family unit, then he will labor to accomplish that.

The divorce rate in the United States has never been higher.[9] I believe this is mostly because of our conditioning and expectations as a society. Divorces occur and then come the remarriages. But are we happy then? Sadly, no. In fact, in second marriages, the divorce rate is even higher than first marriages. This is probably because of the same issue of not being able to find the happiness we feel we deserve. What these people in broken marriages don't understand is that through the trials of marriage, with commitment as a key component, true joy and happiness is always possible and the rewards become immeasurable.

The Lord has said, "And it must needs be that the devil should tempt the children of men, or they could not be agents unto themselves; for if they never should have bitter they could not know the sweet" (D&C 29:39).

Because we have tasted the bitter, we can know the sweet. We can achieve the level of happiness we believe we deserve here on earth. The key word here is *achieve*. Tasting the bitter is part of the equation, the opposite end of the spectrum.

Bruce R. Hafen explained, "In going off to a Church school, joining the Church, marrying, having children, or serving a mission, we must often overcome tremendous odds even to embark upon the experience. For that reason, it is only natural to believe that once we have won the right to the experience, we should live happily ever after."[10]

In my experience as a counselor working with struggling couples, many of them do believe that their marriage relationships should have turned out differently or been easier to manage.

That is not the way the world works. Hafen expresses his disagreement with this assumption,

"He shall consecrate thine afflictions for thy gain." There *is* a link between sorrow, toil, affliction, and "incomprehensible joy." Otherwise, there may only be innocence—"having no joy, for they knew no misery" (2 Nephi 2:23).[11]

Opposition in all things. To experience true joy, we must partake of pain and hardship. Hafen continues,

It is never intended that we should partake of the tree of life and thereby gain full access to perfecting grace *before* we have stumbled and groped and learned all we can from the disappointments and surprises of this vale of tears. I suppose that is why the Lord guarded the way to the tree of life after Adam and Eve had partaken of the first tree: . . . they needed to taste the bitter in order to "prize"—to appreciate, to understand, to grasp the *meaning* of—"the good" (Moses 6:55). Perhaps the essence of that good is the gift of eternal life, which we can only comprehend after we do all we can do. Until we are prepared in what may look like very imperfect ways to receive them, we are not ready for the gifts that perfect our nature.[12]

Mortal life is a test. It is a time for struggling, falling, learning, and developing. Only once we have been instructed can we fully appreciate the boundless blessings that await us:

Without that course of instruction, they could not have developed the capacity to live a meaningful celestial life. So it is with our experience as their children: Mortality is not mere estrangement from God—it is the crucible through which the possibility of truly meaningful life becomes real.[13]

The hardest things in life are often the most worthwhile. It's through opposition and struggle that we develop and have the potential to improve. We need to work through the harder days to get to—and better enjoy—the joyful ones.

Adam and Eve left the Garden of Eden so that "they might have *joy*." Not nice days. Not yawning and stretching and lounging cozily in front of a TV throughout eternity. After Adam and Eve had been in the lone and dreary world long enough to get some idea of what it meant to "eat bread by the sweat of they face" and to "bring forth children in sorrow," an angel taught them the plan of salvation. By then they had enough understanding to appreciate what they were taught. Adam said, "Because of my transgression my eyes are opened, and in this life I shall have joy" (Moses 5:10).

Opposition is a central part of mortal life. . . . It is the difference between being green, untested, and inexperienced versus being ripe, seasoned, tested, and having a mature perspective. As one of Shakespeare's characters in *King Lear* says to his father after they have undergone prolonged, terrible opposition, "Ripeness is all." Ripeness. Fullness. Richness. How different from innocence; for if there is only innocence, there is but little meaning.

The most important things we can learn in this mortal probation are learned the slow way, through practice, through trial and error.[14]

I remember hearing a story about a little boy and a butterfly. One day, a little boy saw a cocoon hanging from the branch of a nearby tree. As he focused on it, the cocoon began to move. The butterfly was beginning to break out of his cocoon. In the little boy's excitement, he waited for the butterfly's release. He became impatient and, in his desire to help the butterfly, he ripped open the cocoon to free the butterfly from his apparent struggle. The butterfly immediately fell to the ground and eventually died.

What the little boy didn't understand is that the butterfly needed to fight its way out of the cocoon. The adversity was necessary for the butterfly to gain the strength to fly. The juices that are necessary for flight are released into its wings during the butterfly's fight out of the cocoon.

There are two types of adversity in this story: the adversity of the butterfly's fight out of the cocoon and the adversity of the young boy having to watch the butterfly struggle. Both are important lessons in life.

In the book of Moses, the Lord is explaining how adversity helps us gain our eternal reward. He said, "They taste the bitter, that they may know to prize the good. And it is given unto them to know good from evil; wherefore they are agents unto themselves. . . . Wherefore teach it unto your children, that all men, everywhere, must repent, or they can in nowise inherit the kingdom of God, for no unclean thing can dwell there, or dwell in His presence" (Moses 6:55–57). By the Spirit we are justified, so His Spirit and light actually has a cleansing, justifying effect on us when it is present. By His blood we are sanctified. There is no other way to dwell in our Heavenly Father's presence than accepting the blood of His atonement in our lives and looking to Him in every thought.

The Lord further explained this concept of sanctification by His blood when he spoke about trials in our lives.

> I, the Lord, have suffered the affliction to come upon them, wherewith they have been afflicted . . . Yet I will own them, and they shall be mine in that day when I shall come to make up my jewels. Therefore, they must needs be chastened and tried, even as Abraham, who was commanded to offer up his only son. For all those who will not endure chastening, but deny me, cannot be sanctified. (D&C 101:2–5)

The adversity each of us has to endure is unique and each of us will be tried as Abraham, not meaning that we will be commanded to offer our children as a sacrifice, but that we will be stretched so far that we don't feel like we can take anymore. The truth is, at that degree of trial, we can't take any more if we're relying on our own power. One of the reasons we suffer adversity, opposition, and temptation may be to realize we absolutely need Jesus Christ and His power and His sacrifice to get us through such times in our lives. And though each of us will have unique challenges, universally we might have similar challenges like the loss of a loved one, opposition from others, personal sin, or a loss in confidence and faith. But Jesus Christ has the power to deliver us from any of those trials, and more specifically the exact trial we are going through if we embrace Him in our lives. By exercising faith and humility, we will naturally be guided to repentance and additional light and truth on how to overcome and be delivered from the trials.

This concept of strength, wisdom, and happiness that can come through adversity applies to all of us. It often becomes frustrating and difficult to struggle through our challenges. That's when we can place the focus on faith and hope, understanding that the Lord is aware of us individually and collectively. True happiness comes from following the Lord and His will in our lives as well as through hard work and commitment to daily living and sacrifices.

7

Personalizing the Marvelous Atonement

How can we personalize the Atonement to help us in our lives? True joy will always come through understanding and using the atoning sacrifice of the Lord. This has been a difficult task for a number of my clients.

Elder Dallin H. Oaks said, "The central idea in the gospel of Jesus Christ—its most powerful idea, along with the universal Resurrection—is the Atonement of our Savior. We are His servants, and it is critical that we understand the role of the Atonement in our own lives and in the lives of those we teach. Essential to that understanding is an understanding of the relationship between justice and mercy and the Atonement, and the role of suffering and repentance in this divine process."[1]

Additionally, Elder Richard G. Scott explained the importance of the Atonement.

> The Redeemer can settle your individual account with justice and grant forgiveness through the merciful path of repentance. Full repentance is absolutely essential for the Atonement to work its complete

miracle in your life. By understanding the Atonement, you will see that God is not a jealous being who delights in persecuting those who misstep. He is an absolutely perfect, compassionate, understanding, patient, and forgiving Father. He is willing to entreat, counsel, strengthen, lift, and fortify. He so loves each of us that He was willing to have His perfect, sinless, absolutely obedient, totally righteous Son experience indescribable agony and pain and give Himself in sacrifice for all. Through that Atonement we can live in a world where absolute justice reigns in its sphere so the world will have order. But that justice is tempered through mercy attainable by obedience to the teachings of Jesus Christ.[2]

The unyielding demands of justice upon those who have violated the laws of God—the state of misery and torment described in the scriptures—can be intercepted and swept away by the Atonement of Jesus Christ. This relationship between justice and mercy through the Atonement is the core concept of the gospel of Jesus Christ.

Elder Boyd K. Packer spoke on the necessity of the Atonement:

Jacob described what would happen to our bodies and our spirits except "an infinite atonement" was made. "Our spirits," he said, "must have become like unto [the devil]." (See 2 Nephi 9:7–10.)

I seldom use the word *absolutely*. It seldom fits. I use it now—twice:

Because of the Fall, the Atonement was *absolutely* essential for resurrection to proceed and overcome mortal death.

The Atonement was *absolutely* essential for men to cleanse themselves from sin and overcome the second death, spiritual death, which is separation from our Father in Heaven, for the scriptures tell us eight times that no unclean thing may enter the presence of God (see 1 Nephi 10:21; 15:34; Alma 7:21; 11:37; 40:26; Helaman 8:25; 3 Nephi 27:19; Moses 6:57).

Those scriptural words, "Thou mayest choose for thyself, for it is given unto thee" (Moses 3:17), introduced Adam and Eve and their posterity to all the risks of mortality. In mortality men are free to choose, and each choice begets a consequence. The choice Adam made energized the law of justice, which required that the penalty for disobedience would be death.

But those words spoken at the trial, "Thou couldest have no power at all against me, except it were given thee from above" (John

19:11), proved mercy was of equal rank. A redeemer was sent to pay the debt and set men free. That was the plan.

Alma's son Corianton thought it unfair that penalties must follow sin, that there need be punishment. In a profound lesson, Alma taught the plan of redemption to his son and so to us. Alma spoke of the Atonement and said, "Now, repentance could not come unto men except there were a punishment" (Alma 42:16).[3]

The Atonement satisfies the punishment and the resulting blessing is our ability to repent.

Again, the Lord is bound by universal laws. There are always two opposite ends of the spectrum. When we look at what Christ did for us in comparison, the atoning sacrifice of the perfect Lord is at one end of the spectrum and justice for our mortality, which includes our imperfect carnal natures, is at the other. We are all at the mortal end where we're stuck without our Savior. Everything good comes from that other end, Christ's end of the spectrum. Our ability to be or do anything good comes from that end of the spectrum, from Jesus Christ. He balances the equation through His sacrifice.

Elder Dallin H. Oaks, regarding this issue, stated, "I conclude with a message of hope that is true for all but especially needed by those who think that repentance is too hard. Repentance is a continuing process needed by all because 'all have sinned, and come short of the glory of God' (Romans 3:23). Repentance is possible, and then forgiveness is certain."[4]

President Kimball said, "Sometimes . . . when a repentant one looks back and sees the ugliness, the loathsomeness of the transgression, he is almost overwhelmed and wonders, 'Can the Lord ever forgive me? Can I ever forgive myself?' But when one reaches the depths of despondency and feels the hopelessness of his position, and when he cries out to God for mercy in helplessness but in faith, there comes a still, small, but penetrating voice whispering to his soul, 'Thy sins are forgiven thee.'"[5]

Christ has always been there, Christ is always there, and Christ will always be there with open arms to embrace us and help us through life's internal and external storms. He would never turn us away. I am sure it saddens Christ when we put ourselves down. We would never talk to anyone the way we talk to ourselves. We need to be able to accept ourselves for who we are now, with all our limitations and weaknesses. We can't heal ourselves of our own sins. It's not possible. Christ is our healer, our Savior; he washes off the layers of filth, the mud of the field, through His atoning sacrifice.

I'd like to relate a personal story of how I began to truly accept the Atonement in my life. I lost my third son, Justin, during labor. The doctors did an emergency C-section but they were unable to save him. The cord was wrapped around his neck, constricting his airway. He was three days overdue and the autopsy showed he was a perfectly formed little infant boy. Because of the nature of the emergency situation, the doctors had performed a rapid C-section, and most likely because it had been a fast surgery, I developed a staph infection in my wound. The physicians had to reopen my wound because it needed to drain and heal from the inside out. The healing process took weeks. I was required to go to the doctor's office daily, then every other day to clean and bandage the wound.

Eventually I was healed physically, but not emotionally. I was traumatized by the whole event. It took me years to get pregnant again. But after I did, I was excited and nervous for the upcoming birth. During my third trimester, I experienced my first panic attack. It was awful. I realized at that time how truly afraid I was regarding the negative possibilities of my impending birth.

My physician was caring, explaining I might have to have another C-section considering the nature of my wound. However, he also explained there was a possibility I might be able to have a normal delivery and birth. That's what I wanted. A C-section is major surgery, with a long recovery time. It uses up a lot of valuable energy to heal. If possible, I wanted that energy to care for my baby, so I was thrilled about the possibility of a normal, healthy delivery.

The day finally came. My water broke and I entered the hospital. I was in labor for many hours, through the evening and all through the night. My uterus was actually damaged from my previous experience and it had the possibility of rupturing, which could cause hemorrhaging and possibly lead to the death of my baby or even me.

I was damaged. There was no way I could accomplish this birth without help. The help of my nurses, the hospital facility and staff, and especially the knowledge and expertise of my physician were all necessary for a successful and healthy outcome. My physician knew the risks well. He was the expert. Because he knew what could happen, he stayed at the hospital during the entire sixteen-hour labor until my son was born. During the nighttime hours, he slept in a room mere minutes away from where I was laboring.

I was doing my job as best as I could do, but it wasn't enough. Because of my imperfection and the damaged nature of my condition, it just wasn't enough. I needed backup to stop the possibility of my death and especially that of my baby's death.

Finally, I was near delivery and my baby's heart rate began to plummet. I cried out for help and my physician was quickly at my side, comforting and encouraging me to push as hard as I could. He said, "The baby's coming; it's almost over." And then my beautiful little boy was born. He was healthy and he was crying. I was immediately in tears. I couldn't imagine a greater reward. He was a treasure beyond my comprehension.

I compare this one experience of my life to what the Savior is doing for me during my imperfect mortal state here on earth. I am damaged from my mortal experiences. I cannot save myself; I have never been able to and I would never be able to, no matter how hard I worked or tried. The reality of me coming here and the possibility of everlasting death and darkness without what my Savior did for me is devastating. He took my place. He literally paid for my death.

Being mortal, I need an expert, like my physician who saved me from the possibility of death during labor. I now need a Savior to save me from spiritual death. I'm totally at His mercy. I'm powerless without Him. He is already the accomplished expert. He has done His work, gone to school, and now He's ready to save me from certain death, as well as everyone else who has inhabited this earth and all of God's creations.

Many times even faithful members of the Church can drift into relying too much on themselves for meeting the challenges of mortality, attempting to perfect themselves. Stephen E. Robinson points out that it is one thing to believe in Christ but another to believe Christ: "Many of us are trying to save ourselves, holding the Atonement of Jesus Christ at arm's distance and saying, 'When I've perfected myself, then I'll be worthy of the Atonement.' But that's not how it works. That's like saying, 'I won't take the medicine until I'm well. I'll be worthy of it then.'"[6]

Our Savior has already given His sacrifice. It's now up to us to accept it. The problem I have seen over and over again is many of us don't. The reality of the Atonement working for us individually is difficult for our human natures to accept and embrace. We often believe we can fix ourselves or we at least have the desire to do so. And many of us believe the Atonement works for others but not for us. Either we believe we've done too much wrong and are too damaged for help or we believe we can fix ourselves. This is simply not true.

In the Book of Mormon, King Benjamin's people desired to be spiritually reborn following their king's teachings in the first few chapters of Mosiah. They too had experienced the mistakes of mortality and were experiencing a struggle to accept the Atonement with faith in Jesus Christ. "And they had viewed themselves in their own carnal state, even less than the dust of the earth" (Mosiah 4:2). But a miraculous thing happened when they turned to Christ's Atonement in faith:

> And they all cried aloud with one voice, saying: O have mercy, and apply the atoning blood of Christ that we may receive forgiveness of our sins, and our hearts may be purified; for we believe in Jesus Christ, the Son of God, who created heaven and earth, and all things; who shall come down among the children of men. And it came to pass that after they had spoken these words the Spirit of the Lord came upon them, and *they were filled with joy, having received a remission of their sins, and having peace of conscience*, because of the exceeding faith which they had in Jesus Christ. (Mosiah 4:2–3; italics added)

All of us can similarly be filled with joy, receive a remission of our sins, and have peace of conscience by accepting the Atonement in our lives.

The prophet Nephi gave us a tremendous example on how to apply this principle of faith in the Atonement. As he was lamenting about his mortal state and began to be overcome by his own emotions, he turned to the Atonement for strength to. He said, "Yea, my heart sorroweth because of my flesh; my soul grieveth because of mine iniquities. I am encompassed about, because of the temptations and the sins which do so easily beset me. And when I desire to rejoice, my heart groaneth because of my sins. . . . O Lord, I have trusted in thee, and I will trust in thee forever. I will not put my trust in the arm of flesh; for I know that cursed is he that putteth his trust in the arm of flesh" (2 Nephi 4:17–19, 34).

It's normal for us to want to save ourselves, to fix ourselves. We want to be able to do something productive following our sinful behavior. This is where repentance can help us feel better. Repentance is looking toward Christ and understanding He paid for our sins already. It's looking to the debtor in gratitude, not the debt.

Because each of us is unique, no two of us will experience the same circumstances in this life, but we will universally need help beyond ourselves. The infinite and eternal sacrifice of our Savior provides the power to deliver us the help needed. He came to know through His experience all our pains, griefs, and weaknesses. The prophet Alma described it this way:

> And He shall go forth, suffering pains and afflictions and temptations of every kind; and this that the word might be fulfilled which saith He will take upon Him the pains and sicknesses of His people. And He will take upon Him death, that He may loose the bands of death which bind His people; and He will take upon Him their infirmities, that His bowels may be filled with mercy, according to the flesh, that He may know according to the flesh how to succor His people according to their infirmities. (Alma 7:11–12)

The Atonement does apply to all. The Savior not only feels grief in a general sense, but he knows *your* personal grief that only you feel. Because He knows your heart, He also knows how to instruct you to heal, if only you exercise your faith in Him and accept His Atonement. If you do, you will be comforted by the Holy Ghost and be filled with joy, receive a remission of sins, and have peace of conscience.

8

Finding True Joy

How do we find true joy? Heavenly Father says it is possible. In fact, that's His desire and purpose for us. "Men are that they might have joy" (2 Nephi 2:25). As mentioned previously, the word *might* is key. It is a conditional action verb, meaning it requires action according to the necessary conditions to be successful. A wise gentleman told me once that the difference between a dream and a goal are action steps. We can dream all we want about being happy and having joy, but until we take the appropriate steps to make it a goal, it will not happen.

Lucifer wants us to believe that joy isn't possible, that it's too hard to achieve. He uses his tools and lies to try to undermine the truth of how to find joy in our lives. Part of the effort required on our part to experience joy is willingness to accept the reality and nature of the world we live in. We live in a trauma-based world filled with trials and adversity. However, we have been taught that adversity is necessary for growth. Our Heavenly Father knows exactly what we need to develop. He is our teacher.

Every trial I have ever been through I can now look back on with recognition of what I learned from them and how I needed that wisdom and knowledge for my next step or goal. I have so much trust in the Lord because of what I have been through and the wisdom I gained, which I needed then and continue to need now. The earth is our classroom where we are required to work hard to achieve wisdom and joy.

Gordon B. Hinckley expressed this concept beautifully,

> Anyone who imagines that bliss is normal is going to waste a lot of time running around shouting that he has been robbed. The fact is most putts don't drop. Most beef is tough. Most children grow up to be just like people. Most successful marriages require a high degree of mutual toleration. Most jobs are more often dull than otherwise. Life is just like an old-time rail journey—delays, sidetracks, smoke, dust, cinders and jolts, interspersed only occasionally by beautiful vistas and thrilling bursts of speed. The trick is to thank the Lord for letting you have the ride.[1]

Of course the Lord knows what trials we need for our individual growth and what we need to do to feel more joy in our lives. He knows there must be opposition for us to recognize our growth, understanding, and wisdom.

We have also learned through the scriptures that "He shall consecrate thine afflictions for thy gain" (2 Nephi 2:2). There is a link between sorrow, toil, affliction, and joy. Otherwise, there would only be innocence, "having no joy, for they knew no misery" (2 Nephi 2:23). What this scripture says is that whatever pain we endure faithfully is for our benefit or gain, with the possibility of increased joy.

Following the Lord's will by living the Gospel brings increased joy, here on earth and in the eternities. The Lord tells us what the fruits of the gospel are in modern revelation. He said, "But learn that he who doeth the works of righteousness shall receive his reward, even peace in this world, and eternal life in the world to come" (D&C 59:23). I think it amazing that through our righteous works we not only receive God's greatest gift, eternal life, but we also receive peace *in this life*. Peace and joy that come from following our Heavenly Father's plan on earth are a blessing we receive based on our faith and works. I have seen this blessing in many people I know, and it hasn't meant that their lives have been easy—in fact, they have all had numerous trials, tribulations, and afflictions—but the blessing consisted of the *feeling of peace* that attended them through these trials. It is a wonderful blessing, one that all of us can receive.

Most don't have trouble recognizing the misery surrounding us because of our trials. We also feel unhappy when we focus on the guilt in our lives because, as we have learned, guilt places the focus on us. As long as we are trying to live the gospel, turning toward Christ with remorse instead of guilt allows for joy to become a possibility in our lives.

What I have found to be helpful with my clients in their desire to recognize joy and find more of it in their lives is to develop a plan for joy, a plan that involves action. Before they begin developing their individualized plan, I give them a recipe for joy.

Joy is something that takes work, like how making bread takes effort on our part. We don't automatically wake up every morning and have warm bread available without putting in the effort required to make it.

The ingredients for joy are as follows:
- 2 cups faith
- 1 broken heart
- 1 contrite spirit
- 1 cup adversity
- Garnish with something you're passionate about as well as serving others
- 1 cup of being still, taking a needed break, and knowing who you are
- 1 cup of living in the moment with those we love
- 1½ cups of acceptance of change and being grateful for it

This simple recipe has the ability to produce magnificent levels of joy, peace, comfort, and a core level of happiness that manifests an amazing amount of confidence and abilities beyond our comprehension. I see it happen every day. An interesting account of this process comes from the record of Alma in the Book of Mormon.

> And it came to pass that the Lamanites said unto him: What shall we do, that this cloud of darkness may be removed from overshadowing us? And Aminadab said unto them: *You must repent, and cry unto the*

voice, even until ye shall have faith in Christ, who was taught unto you by Alma, and Amulek, and Zeezrom; and when ye shall do this, the cloud of darkness shall be removed from overshadowing you. And it came to pass that they all did begin to cry unto the voice of Him who had shaken the earth; yea, they did cry even until the cloud of darkness was dispersed . . . and *they were filled with that joy which is unspeakable and full of glory. And behold, the Holy Spirit of God did come down from heaven, and did enter into their hearts,* and they were filled as if with fire, and they could speak forth marvelous words. And it came to pass that there came a voice unto them, yea, a pleasant voice, as if it were a whisper, saying: *Peace, peace be unto you, because of your faith in my Well Beloved, who was from the foundation of the world.* (Helaman 5:40–42, 44–47; italics added)

Faith

When looking at the recipe for joy and in the example above, notice that the base ingredient is faith. Let's take a look at faith in more depth and what our leaders have taught us regarding this necessary ingredient. In Hebrews, it's said, "Faith is the substance of things hoped for, the evidence of things not seen" (Hebrews 11:1). In Alma, we learn that "faith is not to have a perfect knowledge of things; therefore if ye have faith ye hope for things which are not seen, which are true" (Alma 32:21). Faith is the fabric that miracles are made of. It is the driving force of action that brings joy and blessings in our lives. In the mud field of our earthly journey, it is our constant decision to focus on moving forward because we know Christ is there waiting to cleanse us and bless us. As strong as our faith is, with all the mixed messages attacking it, it can become fragile. In order to remain strong, faith requires constant nurturing. Faith receives this nourishment through continued scripture study, prayer, and the application of His word.

Elder Richard G. Scott explained the following regarding faith:

When faith is properly understood and used, it has dramatically far-reaching effects. Such faith can transform an individual's life from maudlin, common everyday activities to a symphony of joy and happiness. . . . Your exercise of faith in true principles builds character;

118

fortified character expands your capacity to exercise more faith. As a result, your capacity and confidence to conquer the trials of life is enhanced. . . . What are some of the empowering principles upon which faith is based?

Trust in God and in His willingness to provide help when needed, no matter how challenging the circumstance.

Obedience to His commandments and a life that demonstrates that He can trust you.

Sensitivity to the quiet promptings of the Holy Spirit.

Courageous implementation of that prompting.

Patience and understanding when God lets you struggle to grow and when answers come a piece at a time over an extended period.

"Faith is things which are hoped for and not seen; wherefore, dispute not because ye see not, for ye receive no witness until after the trial of your faith" (Ether 12:6).[2]

Hope is a huge component of faith. We have faith that the spiritual things we feel, but that we cannot see, are true, yet we hope eternal happiness will come after everything we can do here on earth. Hope is an integral facet of our faith, and together they help us recognize and feel more joy in our lives. The prophet Moroni confirmed this in his account.

How is it that ye can attain unto faith, save ye shall have hope? And what is it that ye shall hope for? Behold I say unto you that ye shall have hope through the Atonement of Christ and the power of His resurrection, to be raised unto life eternal, and this because of your faith in Him according to the promise. Wherefore, if a man have faith he must needs have hope; for without faith there cannot be any hope. (Moroni 7:40–42)

We have been promised that our ultimate reward of eternal life, following our test period here in mortality, is where we do live "happily ever after" (see D&C 93:45). So maybe if we look at the Cinderella story in a different way, there is some truth to it. When she is going through her trials with her stepmother and stepsisters, she is in the field of mud, trudging toward her goal of eternal life. When she reaches her prince and rescuer (symbolically Christ's atoning sacrifice in our lives), she has the ability to live happily ever after. Happily ever after is a possibility in our next estate.

Having a Broken Heart and a Contrite Spirit

With the next two ingredients for joy, having a broken heart means that you feel broken-hearted that the Savior went through the suffering He did on our behalf and a contrite spirit means that we humbly accept that sacrifice in our lives. In other words it means recognizing the source of all our blessings as coming from Heavenly Father. In one word, humility.

When we are humble and turn our thoughts, actions, and beliefs toward Christ, He will endow us with strength from on high to become who He wants us to become so that we can be filled with joy in our lives. The prophet Moroni described the relationship between faith, hope, and humility when he stated, "And again, behold I say unto you that he cannot have faith and hope, save he shall be meek, and lowly of heart" (Moroni 7:43). Elder Oaks spoke about this condition, stating the following: "When a person has gone through the process that results in what the scriptures call 'a broken heart and a contrite spirit,' the Savior does more than cleanse that person from sin. He gives him or her new strength. That strengthening is essential for us to realize the purpose of the cleansing, which is to return to our Heavenly Father."[3] A person who has repented of his sins will forsake them. Forsaking sins is more than resolving not to repeat them. Forsaking involves a fundamental change in a person, which is a step toward a change of heart and a contrite spirit.

Elder Oaks continues, "King Benjamin's congregation described that mighty change by saying that they had 'no more disposition to do evil, but to do good continually' (Mosiah 5:2). Persons who have had that kind of change in their hearts have attained the strength and stature to dwell with God. That is one definition of what we call being saved."[4]

Ultimately, when we obtain a broken heart and a contrite spirit we can recognize the source of all our blessings because we see that all good in the world comes through Jesus Christ, our Savior. We become humble and teachable. Our daily actions are centered on

Him with His will in mind. Faith and humility in combination are a powerful source for repentance and joy. When we kneel before the Lord with a broken heart and a contrite spirit, the possibility of joy in our daily lives exponentially grows.

Adversity

As much as I might wish otherwise, adversity is a necessary ingredient for joy. We all have to experience some kind of trial in our lives where we feel suffering and pain in order for us to be able to feel joy. It is also symbolic of the great sacrifice that Christ endured on our behalf, which enabled Him to receive His eternal reward.

Enduring our trials well will likewise qualify us for our eternal reward. We have to be willing to remain vulnerable enough for more possible pain to have the chance to feel more joy. Because we don't like pain, many of us withdraw to protect ourselves from further pain, which ironically limits the possibility of additional joy. It's a problem that limits our access to joy in future circumstances without awareness, management, and healing. Peace and joy are always benefits that follow our trials. Christ is where we can find the peace that will carry us through future hardships in our lives.

Elder Jeffrey R. Holland said that

> the search for peace is one of the ultimate quests of the human soul. We all have highs and lows, but such times come and they usually always go. . . . But there are times in all of our lives when deep sorrow or suffering or fear or loneliness makes us cry out for the peace which only God Himself can bring. These are times of piercing spiritual hunger when even the dearest friends cannot fully come to our aid.
>
> Perhaps you know . . . courageous people who are carrying heavy burdens and feeling private pain, who are walking through the dark valleys of this world's tribulation. . . . These beloved people seek the Lord and His word with particular urgency, often revealing their true emotions only when the scriptures are opened or when the hymns are sung or when the prayers are offered. Sometimes only then do the rest of us realize they feel near the end of their strength—they are tired in brain and body and heart. . . . Christ and His angels and His prophets forever labor to buoy up our spirits, steady our nerves, calm our hearts, send us forth with renewed strength and resolute hope.

They wish all to know that "if God be for us, who can be against us?" In the world we shall have tribulation, but we are to be of good cheer. Christ has overcome the world. Through His suffering and His obedience He has earned and rightly bears the crown of "Prince of Peace."[5]

An acronym that helps us to have more joyful experiences in our lives is:

J – Jesus (Follow Him)
O – Only (Jesus Only)
Y – Yield (Turn Away)
F – From (From Lucifer's tactics)
U – Unrighteous (He will deceive and lead us astray)
L – Lucifer (He is our enemy)

Do Something You Are Passionate About and Serve Others

I believe that finding something you are passionate about speaks for itself as an ingredient. When we are involved in something we enjoy doing and see the results of our efforts, we can have a great amount of joy. My husband is passionate about our yard and making it beautiful with waterfalls, fireplaces, and recently a pizza oven where he is determined to become proficient at making all kinds of wonderful artisan breads. He is passionate about it and enjoys everything he is doing. I am passionate about spending time with my grandchildren. There is nothing that brings me more joy than their hugs and giggles and especially their determined jaunts as they forcefully charge across the lawn to knock me over with their bear hugs. In my eyes, nothing could be better.

Have you asked yourself what your passion is? Someone once told me the way to live a long life is to exercise a half hour a day and to have something you are passionate about. It makes a lot of sense.

As for service, naturally serving others takes the focus off of ourselves and places it on Christ as we are helping our Heavenly Father's children. There is no better example of serving others than Jesus Christ Himself. Jesus's own declaration of his Messianic mission was as follows: "The Spirit of the Lord *is* upon me, because he hath anointed me to preach the gospel to the poor; he hath sent me to heal the brokenhearted, to preach deliverance to the captives, and recovering of sight to blind, to set at liberty them that are bruised" (Luke 4:18). He also said, "I am among you as He that serveth" (Luke 22:27). Like Christ, service will give us a sense of joy and satisfaction as we strive to help others through their own journey through the mud field. Serving others can help others understand how we follow Christ.

When we are accomplishing something, service or a passion, we get to see results from our efforts. This is an important part of finding joy and satisfaction from our daily efforts. For example, if we continually play a video game but never win, causes a different feeling than doing something where you see the benefits from your time and effort. It's natural for us to have the desire to gain satisfaction, to want to see the results of our efforts. When we see some concrete and measurable progress from our efforts, joy and satisfaction will naturally increase.

Take Time for Yourself

The sixth ingredient for joy is taking time for yourself, where you can be still once in a while, still enough to maybe truly get to know yourself. The Lord has said, "Be still and know that I am God" (D&C 101:16). Sometimes we believe we need to be constantly doing or accomplishing tasks to live productive lives. I've found with my clients that true healing power comes from simply being still at times.

I believe when we feel this stillness and identify the source, we can feel our connection to the Lord where the possibility of joy is unending and incomprehensible. I've worked with individuals who sometimes have difficulty taking time out for themselves. They feel uncomfortable being still because they don't like the feeling that stillness brings. They have been conditioned to continually serve others but overlook the need to serve themselves. It's a beautiful, righteous goal to serve others, but if we don't take care of ourselves, then we eventually have nothing left to give to others as we become worn down and out.

Christ was serving others on earth, but He also took time for himself by going into the mountains to regroup and to reenergize

Himself, to speak with His Father and consult with Him, to feel of His presence, and to be still (see Matthew 14:23). This is an important lesson we can learn and implement. If our Savior recognized the need to be still, we should take an appropriate amount of time to do something similar. It allows us to enjoy the benefits of long-lasting joy and have the energy to continue on our journey through the mud field. A healthy balance is needed.

Live in the Moment

The next ingredient in our recipe for joy is one we often overlook: the ability to live in the moment. You might be wondering what's so difficult about that. But it is a truly difficult thing to do for many of us because of our conditioning; we can't bear to waste time. We are workers and survivors, taught to accomplish as much as possible in the smallest amount of time. Because of this, we have become excellent multi-taskers. Though this can be a great skill in many different areas, especially employment avenues, this is not a wonderful or ideal trait if you want to have a lot of joy in your life.

Just think about dressing an infant or a young toddler. Your phone rings and you spend the time talking on your phone as you're also dressing your child. During this multi-tasking, you miss the opportunity to connect, in a playful and memorable way, with your young child, like a tickling moment, hugs, or a peek-a-boo game. This is one small instance, but it can add up over the course of time. Unless we consciously combat to do one thing at a time, we may miss out on moments with our loved ones.

Oftentimes, because we have not been taught the importance of living in the moment, or we're uncomfortable being still, we tend to skirt around the moment or miss the moment altogether. I like to give a personal example of how the living in the moment hit me strong one day, years into my life. My mother and father had nine children and I grew up right in the middle of that. My mother came from a nuclear family unit with a sibling group of eleven. I grew up with over a hundred first cousins, so needless to say I wasn't ever alone. I had people around me constantly. I married at the tender age of nineteen and started having children of my own. So then there were more people, not to mention my husband's side of the family.

I have now raised children for thirty-three continuous years until this year, when my youngest son, who is eighteen, moved out of our home to further his education.

What I realized one day, sitting alone and quietly in my living room, is that I hadn't ever truly felt my home before. I've lived in my home for over twenty-four years, but I hadn't ever felt the essence of my home. I had lived under this roof every day with the purpose of accomplishment in mind. I was either coming home from a long day of counseling to check on my children and make sure they were all there and tucked in for the night; or coming home to go to bed myself, or to clean the kitchen, or vacuum, or dust, or read to my kids, or do the laundry, or mop the floors, or call a friend back who had left a previous message, or read the last chapter of a book, or turn off the sprinklers, and so on.

But that day, in my living room, for the first time I was in my home—experiencing my home—without a purpose. I was just there. My home felt different to me. It almost took on its own personality of a sort. It definitely has a unique feeling I hadn't felt before. It was a pleasant feeling, not one of loneliness or sadness or sorrow. It felt so good to be home, simply to be home. That was the moment, that was living in the moment: being home and soaking in the peace of my home, the feeling of my home. I also placed more attention on who I truly am. And it was all right; in fact, it felt good.

It's not always easy to find time to be alone because of busy schedules and responsibilities, but what I have learned from my clients and through my own experiences is that it's worth making time for. At first it may feel uncomfortable and as we practice being in the moment and being still with ourselves, it becomes easier and our desire to have more of this quality time grows. It doesn't take a large amount of time to accomplish. It only takes practice because we are new at the skill.

Being in the moment is exactly the opposite of trying to accomplish great feats or trying to find something where it doesn't necessarily exist. Sometimes we even do tasks to try and cover up what we're truly feeling because it is uncomfortable for us. St. Augustine said, "Men go abroad to wonder at the heights of mountains, at the huge waves of the sea, at the long courses of the rivers, at the vast compass of the ocean, at the circular motions of the stars, and they pass by themselves without wondering."[6]

This quotation reminds me of a conversation I had once with one of my many cousins. He was showing me his bucket list for him to accomplish before he dies. It included a whole page of many fabulous feats including climbing Mount Everest, running a marathon, riding his bicycle cross-country, traveling around the world, and swimming across the English Channel. I was wondering to myself what he wanted his many children to say about him or remember about him following his death. He could be missing out on some valuable in-the-moment experiences with his children or family during his adventures.

Many times we don't want to think about our inevitable deaths, but doing so might help us to understand and accomplish truly meaningful tasks while we are here. I love attending funerals for that reason. I have never heard anyone say anything bad about any deceased individual, and I always learn something valuable and wonderful about that person's life.

One of my favorite funerals was my brother-in-law's, who died suddenly from a massive heart attack. His six children were grown and each of them spoke about him at his funeral. He had five sons and one daughter. Each son spoke favorably about his wonderful father, but his daughter's talk is the one that I remember the most. She explained that every Sunday morning while she was young, she and her father would spend tender moments together reading the comic section of the newspaper. She explained he would lift her up onto his lap and then begin reading the comics aloud. He would then throw his head back and laugh. That is a perfect example of living in the moment. A routine tender moment between a father and daughter, which not only brought them joy, but in her sharing her story I feel joy each time I reminisce about it. Joy is all around us if we do the work necessary to achieve it.

Another way to live in the moment is experiencing emotions, comfortable ones as well as uncomfortable ones, your own emotions as well as others'. Christ taught us to mourn with those who mourn and comfort those in need of comfort (see Mosiah 18:9). We don't do that well as a society and we're missing out on a lot of available joy, unless we become willing to step out of our comfort zone and feel for others and for ourselves.

I remember hearing a story about a young Beehive girl and her advisor at a conference I attended. If any of you have ever worked with Beehive young women, you can understand how excited they get over everything. They enjoy life and have the necessary energy to do it. This young girl's leader was pregnant during the time that she was teaching her. Can you imagine how much fun it would be to watch a Beehive go through this process with her leader? I can imagine all of their young heads and hands glued to this woman's stomach, hoping to hear or feel something.

One day, at the end of the leader's pregnancy, the young woman went to her home to check and see whether the baby had been born. Whoever was at home at that time explained, "Yes, but he was still-born." This young Beehive had no idea what stillborn meant. She ran excitedly back home where her mother was ironing clothes. She exclaimed to her mother that her leader had delivered her baby and it was stillborn.

The girl's mother immediately stopped her ironing, took off her apron, and drove directly to the hospital. She climbed up to the second floor and approached the leader's room. The door was barely propped open. The girl's mother peered into the dark room and noticed her friend lying in the bed, facing away from the door in a fetal position. This woman's immediate response was to turn around and come back later. She believed she had made a mistake by coming and didn't wish to disturb her young friend.

She overcame this resistance, opened the door, and approached her friend. The Beehive leader looked up and tearfully expressed that she felt so empty. The girl's mother climbed into the bed with her friend and they both sobbed and talked for hours.

The Beehive leader related later that this one act of kindness was the most important and beneficial moment that happened during her grieving process. She continued to explain that these few hours with a friend expedited her healing process. I'm sure it also positively affected the woman who was brave enough to push past her comfort zone of wanting to run away from feeling the pain her friend was experiencing for the sake of helping another's healing.

It's normal for us to resist this kind of pain in others and in ourselves. But it's always beneficial and necessary to step out of our comfort zone in order to truly help others. Remember, there is no growth in comfort and no comfort in growth.

So in other words, we need to feel uncomfortable in order to grow. Many times as I work with people, they began to cry. Most of them feel uncomfortable and resist the urge to cry. They apologize for crying. They explain how much they hate to cry. Usually, the main reason behind this is that they feel weak and vulnerable. Vulnerability isn't a comfortable feeling for any human being who has been previously hurt. This is especially true with our past painful emotions we have effectively buried. Emotional expression is necessary to heal from this toxicity and is an indicator that true healing is taking place.

Karol Kuhn Truman, author of *Feelings Buried Alive Never Die*, says, "Of all the languages in the world, the most difficult language to communicate is the language of feelings. One of our greatest challenges as human beings is to effectively communicate with other people what we truly feel. Perhaps the most significant and consequential challenge we face, however, is acquiring the ability to communicate congruently with ourselves."[7]

We need to push beyond our comfort zones and express emotions with others, and especially ourselves, if we want to remain healthy, both emotionally and physically. Bottled emotions are stressful and painful, eventually causing physical illness if not managed effectively.

Karol Kuhn Truman explains the notion further:

What you may not realize is that when negative feelings are not resolved as they occur, these feelings remain very much alive in your physical energy field (body) and these feelings affect each day of your life. . . . These buried feelings are very real. . . . They will make themselves known when you least expect it. These buried feelings may suddenly—after smoldering or fermenting for who knows how long—become apparent in your physical well-being. How? Through dis-ease. Or, the effects of these buried feelings could be exhibited in your relationships. Perhaps these feelings will become evident in your mental, emotional or financial well-being. Take your pick . . . one or all.[8]

Are we willing to step out of our comfort zones and live in the moment with ourselves as well as others? As we heal, will we be willing and able to show more vulnerability? This is where Christ would want us to be as we serve ourselves and others.

Accepting Change

Part of being vulnerable is accepting change and learning to let go of what we believe we have control of but in actuality don't.

Looking back on my experiences with myself and many of my clients, I've seen two commonalities, one being that we as people really like feeling as if we're in control and the other being that we don't enjoy change. Both of these can restrict the amount of joy in our lives, sometimes to a great extent.

For example, I raised all boys and when they became teenagers I explained to them that they were probably going to find ways to do whatever they want to do. I also explained that there would be natural consequences for their actions.

A possible consequence I illustrated to them was if they decided to sneak out each night and party, they'd more than likely be caught by the authorities and have to face the judicial system.

The sense of control that we have to let go of for us to find joy is trying to control things and others that we may not have any control over at all. I could have put bars on my sons' windows, or stayed up every night watching them to make sure they didn't run off, but at some point it would've become too much for me to keep up. It wasn't something I had control of in the first place.

As we let go of the control we don't have and accept that change inevitably comes, we increase the possibility of joy and wonderful, memorable experiences.

President Thomas S. Monson explained with the following the importance of spending quality moments with those we love, accepting change, and being grateful, all essential ingredients for joy:

> I begin by mentioning one of the most inevitable aspects of our lives here upon the earth, and that is *change*. At one time or another we've all heard some form of the familiar adage: "Nothing is as constant as change."

Throughout our lives, we must deal with change. Some changes
are welcome; some are not. There are changes in our lives which are
sudden, such as the unexpected passing of a loved one, an unforeseen
illness, the loss of a possession we treasure. But most of the changes
take place subtly and slowly . . .

Many years ago, Arthur Gordon wrote in a national magazine,
and I quote:

"When I was around thirteen and my brother ten, Father had
promised to take us to the circus. But at lunchtime there was a phone
call; some urgent business required his attention downtown. We
braced ourselves for disappointment. Then we heard him say [into
the phone], 'No, I won't be down. It'll have to wait.'

"When he came back to the table, Mother smiled. 'The circus
keeps coming back, you know,' [she said.]

"'I know,' said Father. 'But childhood doesn't.'"

Stresses in our lives come regardless of our circumstances. We
must deal with them the best we can. But we should not let them get
in the way of what is most important—and what is most important
almost always involves the people around us. . . . Despite the changes
which come into our lives and with gratitude in our hearts, may we
fill our days—as much as we can—with those things which matter
most. May we cherish those we hold dear and express our love to
them in word and in deed.[9]

In Summary

As President Monson mentioned above, joy is truly possible in
this life. Joy comes from turning our lives toward Christ and recognizing our divine nature like Christ and loving others as Christ
taught us to do. Joy comes thought Christ. The ability to do all this is
where true self-esteem and self-worth comes from. "If any man will
come after me, let him deny himself . . . For whosoever will save his
life shall lose it: and whosoever will lose his life for my sake shall find
it" (Matthew 16:24–25).

Our existence here on earth is a wonderful, spiritual journey of
knowledge, faith, and understanding. Remember that we all rejoiced
when we were told we had the opportunity to come to earth. We
knew it would be difficult. We still were delighted to come and
splash around in the mud, so to speak.

I remember being at my maternal grandfather's cabin one summer when I was young. The cabin was in a beautiful prairie with only a few trees. When I was young, there weren't any video games that we could play while we were there. They didn't have a television or even reception for it in that remote area. When we were at the cabin, we played outside a lot. We often collected frogs from a beautiful nearby spring and would have frog Olympics to see which frog could jump the furthest. I couldn't wait to go to the cabin each summer.

One day I was sitting with my grandfather. It was a sad day because it had been raining for days, which made it difficult for us to play outside for any length of time. I will never forget something my grandfather said to me as he grabbed his raincoat to take his daily trek around the cabin land. We'd been discussing the issue of the rain, and as he walked out the cabin door, he looked at me and said, "When it rains, I like the rain."

That statement became a profound learning experience for me as I grew older and understood the meaning behind what he was trying to teach me. I understood that we're in control of our own choices and attitudes about what is given to us in life, regardless of our trials and daily struggles. It's one of the only things we do have control over in life. I treasure the gift of choice and agency. I can understand why we fought for something so wonderful.

This knowledge and understanding helped me often in my life. I remember specifically one day when my sister called me sobbing one night. She'd recently learned her only daughter who had been severely sexually abused had also come down with a disease called rheumatoid arthritis, which can severely cripple a person in its most severe form. She had finished reading a book all about all the possibilities and worst-case scenarios about what could happen with the disease and was uncontrollably crying about the near future. I explained to her that awareness and knowledge regarding potential harm is always good, but I also explained that attitude and focusing on the positive, while living in the moment with her daughter, was essential for her and her daughter to have for them to access the most chances to heal and find positive outcomes with this disease.

I said it would be beneficial for her to wake up every morning and notice all the positive things she can find and the blessings in her daughter's life, to help her daughter focus on the little things that make their lives better daily. My sister has done this wonderfully with her daughter, who is now married with two beautiful children. She lives with a disease that has always been under control and manageable. Attitude and focus on the positive is a helpful and powerful tool to increase joy in our lives as we forge through our mud field journey.

Here on earth we are together, still trudging through the mud toward the garden, looking to Christ with every step, knowing that until we reach the garden we will not be clean. We don't have the access to the water. There is only mud everywhere we step. We don't have to feel guilty for walking in the mud. We don't have to feel guilty for being dirty because we are in the mud. We're supposed to be in the mud. We don't have to feel guilty for not having access to any water because we aren't supposed to have access. We don't have to feel guilty at all.

Feeling remorse is a different story. Remorse along with gratitude are both healthy feelings I hope we can all feel often for the sacrifice Christ made for each one of us individually; feelings of remorse for the fact that we needed the sacrifice from someone so pure. Remorse for the sacrifice He so willingly gave for us because of our mortality and imperfect natures. He chose to be our Savior. He chose to cleanse us with his healing sacrifice, with His purity, with His innocence, with His knowledge, with His Blood, with His Godhood.

Recognizing what Christ sacrificed for each of us, and following what He has asked us to do here on earth, is the key to happiness and joy and to disarming Lucifer in our lives. I believe it will help us daily if we can remember what the Apostle Paul explained in Romans,

> Who shall separate us from the love of Christ? Shall tribulation, or distress, or persecution, or famine, or nakedness, or peril, or sword? As it is written, For thy sake we are killed all the day long; we are accounted as sheep for the slaughter. Nay, in all these things we are more than conquerors through Him that loved us. For I am persuaded, that neither death, nor life, nor angels, not principalities, nor powers, nor things present, nor things to come, nor height, nor depth, nor any other creature, shall be able to separate us from the love of God, which is in Christ Jesus our Lord. (Romans 8:35–39)

Our Savior Jesus Christ has said, "Look unto me in every thought, doubt not, fear not" (D&C 6:36). If we turn our thoughts to Him, our gratitude can be increased as well as our feelings of remorse toward that perfect being. He is willing to wash us softly, lovingly, and individually, no matter how long it would take to get us clean. He is even willing to wash our feet and in-between our toes, where the mud is probably extra thick and hard to reach. We can't do it. Only Christ. How beautiful that He would be willing to cleanse each and every soul. How great must be His love for all of us. He wants us to recognize and "remember the worth of souls is great in the sight of God" (D&C 18:10). That includes you.

Can we see ourselves there with Christ that day when He walked on water, walking on the water toward Him? Can we see ourselves taking our eyes off of Him and falling into the sea, making our human daily mistakes? He grabs our hand like He grabbed Peter's hand, helping us back on top of the water, not chastising us for falling, but helping us to refocus so we can become strong and powerful through Him and His example. What more could we ask for than a god who is there for us *always*? What he asks, the only thing we are asked to do is look to Him, readjusting our sights back to our Savior every time we fall, with every thought and deed. The reward is beyond measure, joy beyond our highest hopes and expectations through His light and love. How great must *be* His love for us, to accept us, never turning us away.

What better way to emulate our Savior in His love and sacrifice and example than by loving Him back? Love Him back by repenting and having faith and humility in His sacrifice. Love Him back by loving others. Love Him back by loving ourselves. For the word of God teaches us, "Beloved, let us love one another: for love is of God; and every one that loveth is born of God, and knoweth God. . . . Herein is love, not that we loved God, but that He loved us, and sent his Son *to be* the propitiation for our sins. Beloved, if God so loved us, we ought also to love one another. . . . We love Him, because He first loved us" (1 John 4:7, 10–11, 19).

Endnotes

Chapter One

1. Russell M. Nelson, "Perfection Pending," *Ensign*, Nov. 1995.

2. Jeffrey R. Holland, "Come unto Me," *Brigham Young University 1996–97 Speeches* (Provo: Brigham Young University, 1997), 189.

3. Elaine Marshall, "Learning the Healer's Art," BYU Devotional, Oct. 2002, 3.

4. http://en.wikipedia.org/wiki/Frontal_lobe.

5. http://en.wikipedia.org/wiki/Egocentrism.

6. Maxine Murdock, "Hope and Healing," *Ensign*, Jan. 1993.

7. Author Unknown.

8. Robert C. Oaks, "Your Divine Heritage," *Ensign*, Apr. 2008.

9. Alifeleti Malupo, "Forgiveness Key to Inner Peace," *The Honolulu Advertiser*, Sep. 1994.

10. Audrey Nelson, "He Speaks, She Speaks," *Psychology Today*, Jan. 2011.

Endnotes

11. http://studio5ksl.com/?nid=54&sid=25404149.

Chapter Two

1. Dieter F. Uchtdorf, "You Can Do It Now!" *Ensign*, Nov. 2013.

2. Ibid.

3. http://en.wikipedia.org/wiki/Laws_of_thermodynamics.

4. Richard G. Scott, "To Heal the Shattering Consequences of Abuse," *Ensign*, May 2008.

5. Spencer W. Kimball, *The Miracle of Forgiveness* (Salt Lake City: Deseret Book, 1969), 344.

6. Spencer W. Kimball, "Jesus: The Perfect Leader," *Ensign*, Aug. 1979.

7. Quentin L. Cook, "Let There Be Light," *Ensign*, Nov. 2010.

Chapter Three

1. Quentin L. Cook, "Let There Be Light," *Ensign*, Nov. 2010.

2. David A. Bednar, "Marriage Is Essential to His Eternal Plan." *Liahona*, June 2006.

Chapter Four

1. Boyd K. Packer, "The Power of the Priesthood," *Ensign*, May 2010.

2. David A. Bednar, "Marriage Is Essential to His Eternal Plan," *Liahona*, June 2006.

3. Jeffrey R. Holland, "We Are All Enlisted," *Ensign*, Nov. 2011.

4. David A. Bednar, "Things as They Really Are," *Ensign*, June 2010.

5. http://en.wikipedia.org/wiki/Butterfly_effect_in_popular_culture.

Chapter Five

1. Bruce R. McConkie, "The Probationary Test of Mortality," *University of Utah Speeches 1982*, Jan. 1982.

2. Neil A. Andersen, "Never Leave Him," *Ensign*, Nov. 2010.

3. Author Unknown.

4. Joseph F. Smith, *Gospel Doctrine* (Salt Lake City: Deseret Book, 1939), 132.

5. Joseph Fielding Smith, *Doctrines of Salvation* (Salt Lake City: Deseret Book, 1954–56), 18.

6. Gerald N. Lund, "I Have a Question," *Ensign*, Aug. 1986.

7. https://www.lds.org/topics/family-proclamation.

8. Robert C. Oaks, "Your Divine Heritage," *Ensign*, Apr. 2008.

9. Ibid.

10. Bruce R. McConkie, *Mormon Doctrine* (Salt Lake City: Bookcraft, 1966), 290.

11. Carlfred Broderick, AMCAP Seminar Notes, Oct. 1983.

12. Ibid.

13. Ibid.

14. Richard G. Scott, "To Acquire Spiritual Guidance," *Ensign*, Nov. 2009.

Endnotes

15. Richard C. Edgley, "Faith—the Choice Is Yours," *Ensign*, Nov. 2010.

16. Oswald Chambers, *My Utmost for His Highest* (Uhrichsville: Utah, Barbour Publishing, 1987).

17. Bruce Hafen, *The Broken Heart* (Salt Lake City: Deseret Book, 1989), 23.

18. Ibid., 45.

19. Author Unknown.

20. Neal A. Maxwell, "Consecrate Thy Performance," *Ensign*, May 2002.

21. Jeffrey R. Holland, "The Best Is Yet to Be," *Ensign*, Jan. 2010.

22. James E. Faust, "The Healing Power of Forgiveness," *Liahona*, May 2007.

23. Jeffrey R. Holland, "Like a Broken Vessel," *Ensign*, Oct. 2013.

24. Rex E. Pinegar, "Let God Judge between Me and Thee," *Ensign*, Oct. 1981.

25. C. S. Lewis, *Mere Christianity* (New York City: HarperCollins, 2001), 225–27.

26. Neil L. Anderson, "What Thinks Christ of Me?" *Ensign*, May 2012.

27. Henry B. Eyring, "The Power of Deliverance," BYU Devotional, Jan. 2008.

28. Robert D. Hales, "Agency: Essential to the Plan of Life," *Ensign*, Nov. 2010.

29. Sheri Dew, *No One Can Take Your Place* (Salt Lake City: Deseret Book, 2004), 11.

30. Thomas S. Monson, "The Race of Life," *Ensign*, May 2012.

31. Jeffrey R. Holland, "The Laborers in the Vineyard," *Ensign*, May 2012.

Chapter Six

1. http://en.wikipedia.org/wiki/cliff_Young_(athlete).

2. *King James Bible Dictionary*: Abraham, covenant of (Sterling).

3. Carol Pearson, *The Lesson* (Salt Lake City: Gibbs-Smith, 2010).

4. Robert D. Hales, "Agency: Essential to the Plan of Life," *Ensign*, Nov. 2010.

5. Bruce Hafen, *The Broken Heart* (Salt Lake City: Deseret Book, 1989), 79.

6. Ibid., 73.

7. Ibid., 53.

8. Ibid., 83.

9. http://www.cdc.gov/nchs/nvss/marriage_divorce_tables.htm.

10. Bruce Hafen, *The Broken Heart* (Salt Lake City: Deseret Book, 1989), 83.

11. Ibid., 76.

12. Ibid., 24–25.

13. Ibid., 41.

14. Ibid., 81.

Endnotes

Chapter Seven

1. Dallin H. Oaks, "The Atonement and Faith," *Ensign*, Apr. 2010.

2. Richard G. Scott, "Finding Forgiveness," *New Era*, Mar. 2010.

3. Boyd K. Packer, "Who Is Jesus Christ?" *Ensign*, Mar. 2008.

4. Dallin H. Oaks, "The Atonement and Faith," *Ensign*, Apr. 2010.

5. Spencer W. Kimball, *The Miracle of Forgiveness* (Salt Lake City: Deseret Book, 1969), 344.

6. Stephen E. Robinson, "Believing Christ," *Ensign*, Apr. 1992.

Chapter Eight

1. Gordon B. Hinckley, "A Conversation with Single Adults," *Ensign*, Mar. 1997.

2. Richard G. Scott, "The Transforming Power of Faith and Character," *Ensign*, Nov. 2010.

3. Dallin H. Oaks, "The Atonement and Faith," *Ensign*, May 2010.

4. Ibid.

5. Jeffrey R. Holland, "The Peaceable Things of the Kingdom," *Ensign*, Nov. 1996.

6. http://www.brainyquote.com/quotes/authors/s/saint_augustine_2.html.

7. Karol Kuhn Truman, *Feelings Buried Alive Never Die.* (St. George, Utah: Olympus Dist., 1991), 1.

Endnotes

8. Ibid., 2.

9. Thomas S. Monson, "Finding Joy in the Journey," *Liahona*, Nov. 2008.

Notes

_____

_____

_____

_____

_____

_____

_____

_____

_____

_____

_____

_____

_____

Notes

Notes

Notes

Notes

Notes

About the Author

Karen W. John was born right in the middle of nine children. During her childhood, she and her family performed by singing, dancing, and playing instruments as they traveled across numerous states and several countries. Doing so helped her develop a great love for diversity and people. Though she loves performing, her ultimate passion—besides her husband of thirty-seven years and her five sons and their families—is learning and using what she's learned to help others progress and grow. She earned her masters degree in social work at Walla Walla College and is currently a licensed clinical social worker. She has years of counseling experience with individuals, married couples and families, and all forms of addicts. She has taught social work classes part-time at BYU–Idaho and often speaks at the university and at ward and stake functions. She currently resides in the Rexburg, Idaho, area.